chris sheryn

RUGBY for real

the common sense training manual

A & C

To WS
And to all the World's other career enthusiasts.
C.S.

First published 2004 by
A & C Black Publishers Ltd
37 Soho Square, London W1D 3QZ
www.acblack.com

ISBN 0 7136 6896 2

A CIP catalogue record for this book is available from the British Library.

Typeset in 9.5pt DIN-regular

Note: Whilst every effort has been made to ensure that the content of this book is technically accurate and as sound as possible, neither the author nor the publishers can accept responsibility for any injury or loss sustained as a result of use of this material.

Text and cover design by Jocelyn Lucas
Cover images © Corbis
Inside photographs © Grant Pritchard; with the exception of pages x, 42 and 162 © Paul Quinn

A & C Black uses paper produced with elemental chlorine-free pulp, harvested from managed sustainable forests.

Printed and bound in Tien Wah Press Pte., Singapore

Acknowledgements

The team would like to acknowledge the kind help and assistance of the following people, without whom this project would have been unachievable:

All at A & C Black for their belief, patience and support.

Adidas Sportswear for their support with the photoshoot.
(For Adidas stockists enquiries please call +44 (0) 870 240 4204)

Eleiko and Specialist Sports for their kind donation of kit for the weightlifting shoot. (Eleiko equipment can be brought through Escape Fitness, on 0800 4585558 or www.escapefitness.com; Specialist Sports can be contacted on +44 (0) 1590 681810)

Grant Pritchard for the great photoshoot, and Paul Quinn for providing the extra rugby photos (tel: 01952 811 961).

And the models (in order of appearance):

Anna Sheryn – Weightlifting and Pilates instructor and member of the Shropshire County Netball squad.

Greg Dunson – RAF 400m and 110m hurdles Champion and the winner of more RAF individual titles than any other athlete on record.

Mick Cartwright – Five times 85kg World Record holder and World Masters Weightlifting Champion (1999 & 2000).

Sue Lloyd – Six times and current English 58kg weightlifting Champion. West Midlands and Great Britain squad member.

CONTENTS

About Lilleshall

The Lilleshall Sports Injury and Human Performance Centre is one of Europe's leading providers of sports science and injury rehabilitation services.

For over a decade, elite athletes, coaches and sporting bodies from around the world have benefited from its state-of-the-art fitness and physiological testing environments, nutritional advice and training prescriptions to help attain goals and maintain peak performance. The interaction of the Centre's physiotherapists and sports scientists is unique in the UK and places Lilleshall at the forefront of elite sports support services.

About the team

Chris Sheryn A highly experienced consultant from the field of international commerce, Chris enjoyed a successful amateur rugby career. A qualified strength development coach, his work with Lilleshall over recent years has helped provide a practical resource for the thousands of sportspeople who have the drive to maximise their potential.

Conrad Phillips Former Great Britain and RAF team coach, Conrad is now a UK athletics coach and a BWLA instructor. He has produced a national medal winner, an international athlete or a British record holder every year since he started coaching in 1969.

Phil Newton Director of the Lilleshall Sports Injury and Human Performance Centre and a Chartered and State Registered Physiotherapist. Specialising in sports injuries and rehabilitation, he has worked with elite athletes from many sports for over 15 years.

Pauline Newton A Chartered and State Registered Physiotherapist, Pauline has an impressive background in injury rehabilitation – indeed, few in the UK have more experience of helping athletes return to competitive action. Pauline's most recent experience has seen her emphasise contact sports while maintaining her work with international racquet sports squads from around the world.

Sam Howells is a graduate of Loughborough University and holds a BSc in Physical Education and a Masters Degree in Sports Science. A much-published writer on many areas of sports science, Sam has a high level of experience acquired through supporting many elite athletes in a variety of sporting arenas.

Foreword

Rugby is arguably one of the most demanding of sports as it requires a much wider degree of conditioning than do many other activities. Indeed, given an infinite amount of time and energy, the modern player would train for the flexibility and strength of a gymnast, the power of an Olympic weightlifter, the speed of a sprinter and the aerobic capacity of a swimmer.

In a game as technically demanding as ours, the problem of limited training time is not restricted to the amateur ranks and coaches and players at all levels constantly strive for the maximum return on the effort and time invested.

In the top echelons, specialists from a variety of fields combine to create an infrastructure that allows players to focus their attention almost exclusively on the furtherance of their game. But for the thousands of players who do not have the luxury of such time and support, there is always likely to be tension between sport, home and work. I believe that the way in which the team at Lilleshall has addressed this issue will be of great value to players seeking to develop the physical conditioning aspects of their preparation for Rugby.

Sir Clive Woodward

How this book works

No doubt that you will have read, or at least seen, a number of publications that promise to transform your body into that of a world-class rugby player with the absolute minimum of effort . . . **This is not such a book**.

Perhaps you have read the books that describe in endless detail what to do with your eight-hour training days and discuss the importance of a steamed fish and broccoli diet? . . . **This is not such a book**.

This book is aimed at the person who enjoys rugby as just one part of a varied life. You may have to balance family and working commitments with your sport. Until now, it has been difficult to decide exactly what to do with the time you have available to commit to preparation for rugby – it is this question of how to get maximum 'bang for your buck' that this book addresses. It is a concise reference for those who want information they can quickly understand and then use in their quest to ensure they get all they want out of their game. It is designed to give you an edge. And it is important to note that you will not find pages of team or squad drills – this book is about *you* and *your* preparation for *your* sport.

At the Lilleshall Centre we have been working with professional and elite amateur athletes for many years and it is this experience that is behind the structure of the book you are about to read. Our approach is not one that will be found in many other books, and it will not suit everyone. If, however, by the time you finish reading we have you thinking about how you structure your approach to your game, then you will be travelling in the right direction.

What you will find in this book

This book is composed of distinct modules and it is vital that each area is treated with equal importance and that you do not skip to the bits you think are important. Think of the book as an architect's plan for a house build. Like any building project it starts with a ground survey (to ensure that the house will stay up). Next, much of our time is spent on foundations and footings. Once these are in place and sound, then – and only then – can the walls and roof go up. Then, after that, we'll turn our intention to 'interior design' – the nutrition you will need to help you maintain a strong 'structure'.

There are no shortcuts – skimp on the foundations at your peril. Those who do are the ones that keep our injury clinic fully booked ...

What you will not find in this book

Recipes. This is not a cookbook of prescribed workouts and routines that are to be followed rigidly. Each player is different, starts from a different base and has their own particular exercise and conditioning needs. You will therefore be required to use the building blocks that are provided to construct your own programme.

How this book breaks down

1: SURVEYING THE GROUND - YOUR TRAINING TOOL KIT

Here you will be introduced to the tools that will be used in later stages. These include the basic ground rules for success, as well as self-assessment tests that will help you measure where you are now and how you progress.

2: LAYING THE FOUNDATIONS – PHYSICAL ASSESSMENT

This chapter deals with establishing a solid base on which to build. By the end of it, you will have physically assessed yourself and will be more aware of any areas of weakness that need to be addressed.

3: BUILDING ON SOLID GROUND – BEST PRACTICE

This chapter will help you to understand the basics behind the methods and exercises we will use to build towards success.

4: WALLS, ROOF AND WINDOWS – PUTTING IT ALL TOGETHER

This is where you do the real work. There are three distinct and progressive phases to this chapter, which work towards the beginning of your season.

5: INTERIOR DESIGN – DIET AND NUTRITION

This chapter will help you to understand the important link between what you put into your body and what you get out of it.

'TOP TIPS' AND 'MYTH BUSTERS'

You will also find 'Top Tips' and 'Myth Busters' scattered throughout the text. These are tricks that have been gleaned from the professional ranks and the truths behind some of the received 'wisdom' that litters gyms and training pitches.

1 SURVEYING THE GROUND Your training tool kit

aim: to supply you with a set of tools and tactics that can be employed to set and attain your personal sporting goals, including:

- the basic 'golden rules' for success
- self-assessment tools
- details of how to achieve a solid base on which you can build.

Before you start

Preparation and conditioning can and should be enjoyable and interesting; neither one need be a chore. A guide like the one you are holding can show you how to improve your training but this collection of paper, in itself, will do nothing for you. In order to get the most from this book there are three golden rules that must be observed, as outlined below.

Golden rule 1: honesty

Ever heard the expression 'In like a lion, out like a lamb'?
Many people go into a new programme full of energy and enthusiasm, all guns blazing, but that feeling is quick to wane when they find they have set themselves

unrealistic targets. If you can be honest with yourself about what you want to achieve and what time you are prepared to invest, then you have already taken a positive and one of the most important steps.

So, your first task is to evaluate *realistically* how much time you can spend and where it is going to come from. There is no point in setting unrealistic targets that are unachievable. The majority of rugby players must balance work, social life and family commitments with training and playing. If you begin without thinking about a realistic balance, then you will not stick to your programme. This is the road to guilt and disillusionment.

Recognise the following scenario?

> *Day one: Right! This is it – the big push for the new season. I'll get up at five every morning, run for an hour (that'll set me up for the day) and that'll leave the rest of the day free to plan my steamed fish and broccoli diet and my ten sessions at the gym ...*

> *Day two: [The alarm goes off at five] I'm a bit stiff after yesterday – best not do too much too soon. I'll skip the run and do double tomorrow ...*

By somewhere between days three and five you have talked yourself out of the early-morning run in the rain and by round about day six you are comfort-eating because you have let yourself down again ...

Never fear. You are not alone. Help is at hand.

The good news is that it is not impossible to achieve a sustainable balance and remain motivated. There are tricks that can be employed to help you, but from this point on you must be prepared to be brutally and consistently *honest* with yourself. If you are not prepared to do so then put this book down and get a beer out of the fridge – your interests lie elsewhere. And that really is OK – just don't kid yourself, or others, that you would do more 'if only ...'. That is just one short step away from 'You know, I could have gone all the way when I was younger ...', and there is at least one of those guys propping up the bar in every clubhouse, in every sport in the world.

Golden rule 2: pace yourself

Prepare to succeed. Most players have encountered and endured the nightmare of pre-season training that owes more to the Foreign Legion than a scientific approach to sports-specific conditioning. Five-mile runs, hundreds of press-ups and dwindling attendance figures at training sessions by September.

'To train without pain is to train in vain ...'

Pain only means one thing – it's your body's way of telling you that you shouldn't be doing what you're doing! If you are in pain you are pretty likely to be on the verge of injuring yourself and the next visit you'll be making will be to the physio or the doctor, not the gym. No, exercise shouldn't be easy and a little bit of discomfort is to be expected if you are doing things properly. Common sense dictates what is discomfort caused by fatigue and what is pain.

This type of trial by ordeal will be noticeable by its absence from this book. There is a different and much more effective approach, and it is all about planned progression.

In brief: 'Try exercise A. When you can complete that, go to exercise B, which will be more intense' ... and so on. Not new and certainly no more than common sense – so why aren't you doing it?

Some of the worst injuries treated at the Lilleshall Centre are directly attributable to short-cuts. A good example is athletes undergoing intensive plyometrics routines when they have trouble supporting their own weight on one leg (this is no exaggeration)!

Just like a house, you will only be as good as your foundations. So although many of the exercises that follow may appear to you to be very low-level and easy, *do not assume that they are beneath you* because, just like foundations, you skimp on them at your peril.

Consider the rugby myth/legend about Bobby Windsor (if you are Welsh; however, the same legend probably applies to Colin Meads if you are from New Zealand, Ian McLaughlin in Scotland, and so on) whose training consisted of carrying two newborn lambs around a field, one under each arm. This was repeated every day until the sheep were fully grown.

This is classic example of planned progression training. Start small, form a base *with excellent technique* and what is built will be standing on solid foundations. When you plan your training using objectives you can start to see the bigger picture – your long-term strategy – and you will find that impatience disappears. You know where you are going and how today's training is contributing to the journey.

Try another metaphor. Think of your training as a ladder and your goal as the wall it is leaning against.

Only a fool sets the ladder on soft or uneven ground, and you never see anyone jump on halfway up! They all check to make sure that the ladder is secure and step back to see that the ladder is going to take them to the correct part of the wall before they step on to the bottom rung. The ladder has evenly spaced rungs to ensure swift but manageable progress towards the top; no one takes more than one rung at a time and everyone will look at the next rung but will occasionally look to the top to remind themselves of their objective. And without the wall – your goal – the ladder lies on the ground and loses all relevance.

When you are clear about your destination, patience will automatically follow. From time to time you will still be feeling strong at the end of a session – the common mistake is to do just one more rep or lap and keep going until you reach absolute exhaustion. Don't punish yourself for feeling good – if you have planned to do five sets, do five sets – not six – just make a note in your diary and plan to do six next time. In this way you are constantly, but realistically, challenging yourself. You will soon find yourself eager to get back because there was a bit left in the tank last time and you could have done that ninth long-arm pull-up.

Accepting this principle of planned progression is at the core of staying motivated.

Golden rule 3: quality before quantity. Always!

This rule applies equally if you are training on your own or in a group.

A vet once said, 'There is no such thing as bad dogs – only bad owners.' The same can be said of coaches. There are few really bad coaches, but there are numerous competent coaches who are made to be 'bad' because the people working with them consider that just turning up to training is enough, and that their own concentration, attitude and application is incidental.

The coach – whoever they may be – can only offer guidance and set up an environment for practice. The really good coach can diagnose faults and put together practices to fix them. But if the individual chooses to operate within that environment at less intensity or at a lower quality than is required, then it's a wasted exercise for all concerned.

To reiterate: this is the same whether you are training on your own or as part of a group. You must concentrate on quality of exercise at all times. Remember – clichés are sometimes where the truth lies:

Train hard, win easy

If you train at half pace you will play at half pace

But probably most true of all is:

Practice does not make perfect; it makes permanent

That is, if sloppiness is part of your training regime it will become ingrained in your performances.

Reminder

There are three golden rules.

1. **Honesty**: this is *your* rugby career (at whatever level) and the competition is ultimately with yourself.

2. **Pace yourself**: steady and consistent progression is the key; be patient – short-cuts lead straight to the physio's bench.
3. **Quality *always***: excellence is a habit and if it is the standard in your training then this can only have a positive effect on your game.

(Self-) motivation

If it was easy then you wouldn't have bought this book.

Motivational factors will be different for everyone. However, there are certain tricks and tactics that can help when the first pre-season flush of enthusiasm has waned and the alternatives to a cold, wet road or the gym are looking mighty warm and attractive. Read this section and think about how the points it makes might apply to you. Then try them out.

The keys to remaining motivated can be broken down into three distinct areas:

1. setting objectives
2. managing resources (in this case, time)
3. measuring progress against plan.

With the correct approach, you can turn your own sports preparation into a project or hobby rather than a chore that has to be endured. After all, we aren't getting paid for this – it's OK to enjoy yourself!

Before you start you will need:

- a **stopwatch** (as cheap as you like)
- access to a **weights room** (don't worry if you don't have this – there are alternatives and we will look at them later)
- a **diary** (ideally one that has a page per day – it will be your record and your conscience).

top tip An ordinary hardback notebook will do as a training record but a diary is a thousand times better. The reason for this is simple – you only have one set of time so why have two diaries? Most people have one wallet because they have one lot of money; a decent-sized, page-a-day diary will allow you to organise work, training records, social life and family commitments all in one place.

Objective setting

If you have no idea of where you want to go, how will you know when you get there?

Objectives – any objectives (be they work or play) – for you as an individual or for the group of which you are a part must follow some simple rules if they are to be effective. Effective objectives are often described as 'SMART'. This means they are always:

- **S** specific
- **M** measurable
- **A** achievable
- **R** realistic
- **T** timed.

It is perfectly acceptable to set an overall objective that is quite wide, but if you are serious about achieving a goal then you must follow the rules.

For example, a 'general' objective might be: 'I want to improve my speed.' It becomes a SMART objective when you say: 'Between the end of this season and the start of the next I want to be able to run 6 x 30-metre sprints, from a standing start, in under five seconds with a one and a half minute recovery between reps.'

S specific: 'I want to improve my speed over short distances, e.g. 30 m.'

M measurable: '... 6 x 30-metre sprints, each in under five seconds'.

A achievable: e.g. 'I can currently do three reps without rest at this pace.'

R realistic: i.e. the improvement is realistic (only you can tell this).

T timed: 'Between the end of this season and the start of the next ...'.

An example of an un-SMART objective would be: 'I'm going to get myself really fit for next season.' It's non-specific, immeasurable, not timed and unlikely to be realistic. What does 'really fit' mean? How will you know if you have achieved your objective if you can't measure it and cannot specify exactly what you want to achieve?

You should also avoid negative targets, such as 'losing weight', as these are not tangible and it's therefore difficult to convince yourself that you have achieved anything. Figure out why you want to lose weight (or do you really mean fat?) and use that as the target – the loss of weight is a means to an end, not an end in itself. Please under no circumstances pin pictures of yourself looking fat on the beach last year to the inside of the biscuit barrel cupboard – this will merely ingrain a poor self-image. Much more effective are positive, dynamic, focused thoughts. Give yourself a break – you are human after all. Ditch the podgy photo and think out something more positive instead. An example might be: 'My target is to be able to achieve four miles inside 35 minutes while keeping my heart rate within "steady state". I will achieve this by 1st May.' The by-product of a large amount of steady-state training will be fat loss, if combined with the moderation of your diet (more on this later ...). As mentioned above, the fat loss becomes a means to an end rather than an end in itself – trust us, it's a heck of a lot easier that way.

The trick to major improvements is to break down the overall objective into smaller stages with short-term objectives. In this way you can see yourself progressing and you have more chance of staying motivated. These stages are best kept to two or three weeks at the most, otherwise the target will seem too distant and disillusionment can easily set in.

When you set objectives, plan to reward yourself when you achieve them (for instance, buy a special bottle of beer and keep it in the fridge ready for when you bench-press 90 kg for the first time or when you get under 30 minutes for that stamina run).

top tip When you are setting objectives that will run over a long period, measure the time in days rather than weeks or months: 90-day goals somehow sound a lot nearer than three months or 'in the next quarter'. And make sure you have an end date on which you will assess your success. If you set 90-day goals you can then break them into weekly and daily tasks.

Finally:

write the objectives down (in your diary) and tell someone close to you about them – it helps.

When seeking to set achievable goals it is very important that you assess where you are now and, consequently, what areas you need to work on. We'll look at how to measure your current strength, speed and flexibility later. From there you can build your own programme and objectives.

Time management

You can waste money, water, even breath – the only resource that can never be replaced is *time*.

Bearing in mind the life balance discussed earlier, time management is going to be the key to the sustainability of your programme. If you have set your short- and medium-term objectives but have been unrealistic about the time you can comfortably invest in them, then your efforts are doomed before you start. *This is where personal honesty is the key*. The trick is to look at your current commitments and see where you can realistically grab time. The time you will need can be divided into two parts.

1. **Quality time.** This will be the one, two or three evenings a week that you spend at the gym, track or the club. In order to ensure that even these sessions do not become a burden, plan your work. For example, make sure that you plan your sets in the weights room before you get there, then get in, do them and get out. Otherwise what should be a one-hour session can easily turn into a two-hour drudge and, before you know it, your evening is totally wrecked. Gyms are full of chatterboxes; be aware that you will reduce the effectiveness of the time you spend there by becoming one of them.

   If you have family or girlfriend/boyfriend commitments, make sure that your partner is part of your planning process. There is no point planning to go to the gym only to find out that she/he-who-must-be-obeyed is going out and leaving you to baby-sit. Obvious, yes, but many people are guilty of falling into this trap.

2. **Dead time.** This can be used as a supplement. Some examples of dead time and how it can be utilised are as follows:

- **Lunchtimes at work** – if you have a shower, how about getting out on the road? A half-hour run followed by a shower will still have you back at your desk/bench within the hour. No shower at work? Where is your nearest sports centre? They have showers.
- **While the kettle is boiling for your morning cuppa** – make it your routine to do press-ups, ab curls and pull-ups while you wait?
- **Him/Her Indoors left me to baby-sit** – get your 'Martini gym' out (see Chapter 3) or do some skipping.

top tip When you have identified your blocks of time, mark them out in your diary a week in advance and then make *timed* appointments with yourself and stick to them as strictly as you would an appointment with your boss. Planning on a weekly basis will help to avoid hijacking by unexpected events that may take precedence. Also, try to find a training partner who has similar commitments to you as this will aid your self-discipline.

Injuries – and how to deal with them

Steady, progressive training with correct technique will give you the best chance of avoiding injuries. However carefully you prepare, you are still likely to pick up the odd knock or twinge, so it is worth knowing more about the topic of sports injuries.

What are they?

Injuries come in many shapes and sizes. The blister that gives you a bit of a limp, the sprained ankle that keeps you out of action for a couple of weeks, and the completely torn knee ligaments that require major reconstructive surgery.

To help you to decide how to deal with the injuries that will inevitably occur through playing rugby, the following simple classification is a good starting point: *injuries are either due to trauma or to overuse*.

Traumatic injuries are easy to identify as there is a definite cause and effect (for example, an opponent's knee smacking into your thigh and giving you a 'dead leg'). In contrast, overuse injuries are often difficult to diagnose and to treat. Traumatic and overuse injuries usually have one thing in common: pain. With traumatic injuries pain is usually acute and limits function (a 'dead leg', for instance, causes you to limp). Overuse injuries tend to give a more chronic, dull ache, which may come on during exercise but is often worse after activity and even at rest (night pain).

What pain can I train through and when should I just stop?

Pain is a warning sign of tissue injury and requires the modification of exercise and sport, or even complete rest. Minor pain and discomfort that doesn't get worse with exercise, and that gradually eases over a few days, indicates the presence of a minor problem. It may well be possible to play with such symptoms, but the golden rule is that basic exercise function isn't impaired – that is, there is no visible effect on your sporting performance (such as a limp).

Irrespective of pain levels, *all* injuries to the head, neck and spine should be medically checked out (your union will have specific guidelines on head injury). The same goes for any high-speed impact injuries, particularly if significant swelling results.

Does your team have a qualified first aider? If not, then get one. It could save your life. Sports first aid training advice can be obtained from the National Sports Medicine Institute (NSMI), see www.nsmi.org.uk; there are also some useful links on our website: www.lilleshall.com.

First aid – what you can do yourself

RICE is an acronym that spells out a safe and effective remedy for all soft-tissue injuries. (An example of a soft tissue injury is a sprained ankle.) It is made up of the following components:

R = rest

I = ice

C = compression

E = elevation.

Rest

Don't do any more damage. Take complete rest ... that includes dancing!

Ice

The application of ice helps to reduce internal bleeding and relieve pain. Apply ice for 10-minute periods every two to three hours for the first 48 hours. Longer periods of ice application will actually accelerate the circulation, so don't overdo the timing.

Compression

This limits swelling and bruising. Make compression firm but not tight. Use crepe bandages or tubular elastic bandages. Make sure that circulation to the fingers and toes is not restricted by any compression bandages that are too tight.

Elevation

Elevation reduces local blood pressure and helps reduce swelling. Keep the injured part higher than the level of the heart as this will reduce blood pressure at the site of the injury and help control swelling. So, for an ankle injury for example, raise the foot so that your 'toes are as high as your nose'.

RICE is the recipe of choice for the first 24–48 hours following an injury. If pain and swelling are not showing significant improvement after this period, seek medical attention.

Rehabilitation

If you sustain a minor injury then a good place to start your rehabilitation is back at the simple tests that will be outlined in the following pages. These will test your flexibility and body weight control. If you can do these as well as you could prior to your injury, then phase back gradually into light activity and short sessions until you have built up your ability to train normally again.

It is important that you are responsible and disciplined in your approach to injury management. Rushing back before you are ready will certainly leave you frustrated and can easily lead to further injuries. Bear in mind that if you have not been able to train for a significant period, you will need to recover fully and then work back to *full* fitness to give yourself a fighting chance of avoiding further problems.

Eagerness to get back on the field following injury is totally understandable, but in retrospect it will seem ridiculous that you were not prepared to invest a couple more weeks to ensure 100 per cent recovery. It is hard, but try to be disciplined – you will thank yourself in the long term.

Where can I get advice?

If you have sustained a serious injury then it is essential to get a medical opinion (from your GP, club doctor or the local hospital). If you are not able to see a doctor then see a properly qualified (i.e. Chartered) physiotherapist who will help you to decide whether or not you need to see a doctor. (Look for the letters MCSP or SRP after their name; these stand for Member of the Chartered Society of Physiotherapy and State Registered Physiotherapist, respectively.) A physio will be able to guide you through your rehabilitation and get you back to playing fitness as quickly and as safely as possible.

'The more I sweat, the more weight I will lose ...'

True, when you sweat you lose weight. But this weight loss is simply body water loss and you will put it back on as soon as you rehydrate. The only way to lose weight is to use more calories than you consume – pure and simple. The people working out in their waterproofs and with bin liners under their kit are simply making the work a lot harder for themselves and risking the detrimental side-effects of dehydration.

2 LAYING THE FOUNDATIONS
Physical assessment

aim:

- To enable you to assess your physical competence and make you more aware of any areas of weakness that need to be addressed.
- To give you an understanding of the methods we will use to develop such areas.

Before you start

If you are motivated enough to buy this book in order to improve your game, you are probably already champing at the bit to get stuck in. *Hold your horses!* You do not have all the information yet.

You may be tempted to skim through the next few pages and feel that you know 'all that stuff' or that it is 'beneath you' – please assume nothing. By taking the time to read through everything in sequence you will, at worst, reconfirm the presence of your good habits and, more than likely, you will find that well-worn practice is not always the best practice.

The information in the coming pages deals with six specific areas that fit together to help you develop all areas of your game:

- initial self-assessment (to see where you are now)
- stretching and warming
- strength training with weights (to get stronger)
- cardiovascular conditioning (to help you keep going longer)
- speed work (to get you there more quickly)
- diet and the role of supplements (some myths exploded and some realistic advice on ways to refuel).

As you read through, remember the golden rules we introduced you to in the previous chapter:

1. **honesty** – there's no one else around to impress by cheating
2. **pace yourself** and build the intensity of your sessions gradually
3. **quality** – *always*.

This chapter has one more rule for you – let's call it the silver rule:

4. **variety** – keep varying your sessions.

It is easy to become bored with training (usually when it is carried out in isolation and is not part of a larger, longer-term plan). Remember that it's OK to enjoy yourself. Build up a repertoire of routines and rotate them to keep your training varied. Intersperse a hard session with a soft session, a hard week with a soft week, and so on.

Be creative. For example, if you are in a bit of a rut at the gym or on your stamina runs, then simply try combining the two every now and then. Perhaps find a wood to run through and there you will find logs to lift, (strong) branches to use for pull-ups, hills to sprint up, and so on.

Initial self-assessment

To get the most out of your training it is vital to know the point from which you are starting. With a fixed and measurable starting point you can target your efforts and gauge your progress.

Please do the tests that follow *in order* as they are, in themselves, progressive. If you cannot complete (*perfectly*) any of the tests, you should see this as a warning that you have an area of weakness to address. If you skip any then you may end up on the physio's bench as you could be asking your body to compensate for a weakness you didn't know you had. For example, it is not uncommon for a bad back to be caused by all sorts of problems elsewhere: weak abdominals, one leg stronger than the other and so on.

You wouldn't see a pilot take off without checking the aircraft over, so why wouldn't you take time to check yourself out properly? The areas you are going to check out now are:

- legs (basic strength and stability tests)
- legs (relative strength tests)
- abdominals (basic strength and stability tests).

Leg strength and stability

This section will look at how stable your legs are. This information is vital and, before embarking on any heavy strength work, it is important that you check out some basic body weight control movements. If your muscles struggle to control your own body weight, then it makes no sense to load them with extra resistance in the form of free weights or machine weights.

This is particularly important if you have suffered from a lower-limb injury in the past, which could have led to some muscle weakness or imbalance.

The three simple tests are:

- the side step
- the sit to stand
- the bum lift.

They will take you about 10 minutes in total, but will save you a world of problems later as they will highlight any inherent weaknesses.

Side step

How to do it

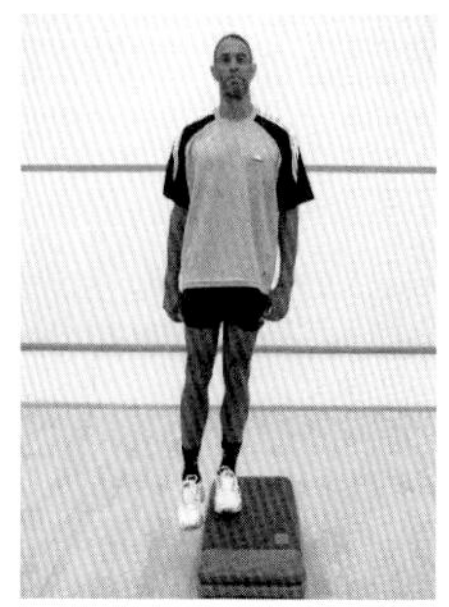

Stand sideways on a bench that is around two-thirds of the height of your shin (measured while wearing your trainers). Keeping the heel of your test leg on the bench at all times, slowly lower the heel of your other foot to the floor. Touch the floor gently with your heel and return, slowly and smoothly, to the start position. You must keep the knee of your test leg in line with the middle of your test leg foot throughout. Repeat with the other leg and compare the two.

Problems?

The most common problem is a case of the wobbles: the knee of your test leg flicks from side to side, producing a jerky movement. Practise by dropping down to the point where you begin to lose control and then step back up. As your control improves you can step deeper.

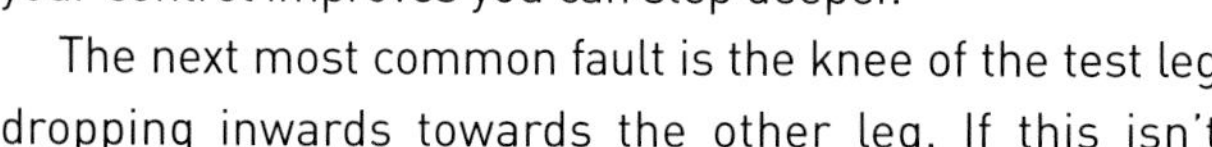

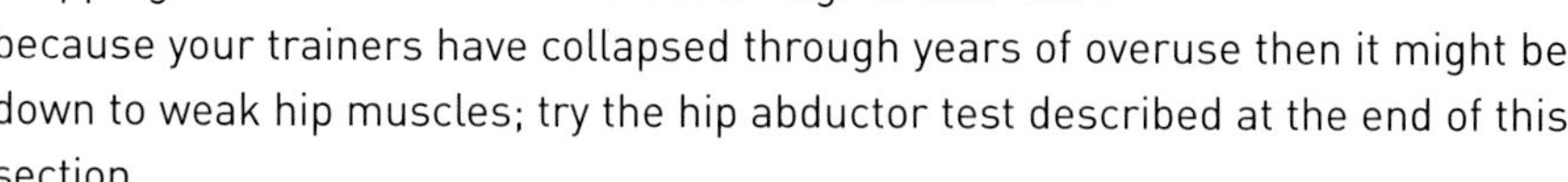

The next most common fault is the knee of the test leg dropping inwards towards the other leg. If this isn't because your trainers have collapsed through years of overuse then it might be down to weak hip muscles; try the hip abductor test described at the end of this section.

Another common fault is an inability to retain control through the full range of movement. This is what is happening if you 'drop' the last two/three inches to the floor as your test leg fails. A good tip is to do the exercise to some suitably steady music, listen to the beat and use it to ensure that the full movement is done at a perfectly consistent pace.

Sit to stand

How to do it

Sit on a dining chair (with a maximum knee-bend angle of 90 degrees), with your arms folded, one foot flat on the floor and the other held up off the ground. Lean forwards and slowly stand up on your test leg (the one whose foot is touching the floor). Keep the knee of your test leg over the foot throughout. Fully straighten the knee and then return slowly to the seated position. Repeat on the other leg and compare the two.

Problems?

Again the most common problem is the wobbles: the test leg knee jerks around uncontrollably. Try using a higher seat (or add cushions to raise the height). As your control improves you can revert to the original seat height.

As with the side-step test, you might find that the knee of your test leg drops inwards towards the other leg. Again, this could be down to weak hip muscles, so try the hip abductor test described at the end of this section.

Core stability

If you haven't noticed, there are two major parts to your body: upper and lower. In many sports – and rugby is one of them – the power that is delivered by the upper body is to a large extent generated by the lower body (the legs). Unfortunately, the conduit of the power generated by these largest muscle groups is one of the most vulnerable sections: the abdomen, your mid-section.

Think of your abdomen as a corset of muscle that has four main sections: the front, the two sides and the back. These sections work together as a team and no one section should be emphasised above any other (although you are unlikely to get comments about your nice back muscles when you are on the beach ...).

Bruce Lee was a great believer in the importance of the abdomen in the delivery of strength, and spent a long time working on it. This 'core' is seen as equally important today and the current vogue is for core stability training. This is nothing new, of course, but it's a great way to sell equipment to those seeking a short-cut. One of the current exercise fads is to use a big gym ball (or Swiss ball) to train the trunk muscles. Be careful when using these; remember golden rule 2: *pace yourself* – progress slowly and consistently. The aim of the gym ball is to destabilise the abdomen and, by putting it under stress, to develop the supporting muscles. This is fine in theory, but if you do not have a good basis of strength to start off with (your 'foundations'), you are heading for a fall.

There are a couple of simple tests you can do to assess how well your trunk muscles work as a team to support your spine. You should be able to do the following exercises well before contemplating the more demanding gym ball routines. Having said that, a good free weights programme together with sensible trunk conditioning work will significantly improve your core stability.

Your 'neutral spine' position

You will see the term 'neutral spine' used a lot in this book; it is an important concept as it is the best position for your back to receive weight. Concentrate on your position when you have completed the following exercise and remember it so that you can return to the same state at any time.

If you are a forward then you (perhaps unwittingly) already know about this principle. The correct pushing position – the one where coaches scream 'Flat back!' or 'Get your position lower!' – is all about positioning your back in such a way that it is safe for it to receive weight.

How to do it

Lie flat on your back with your knees bent and the soles of your feet on the floor. Place the palms of your hands

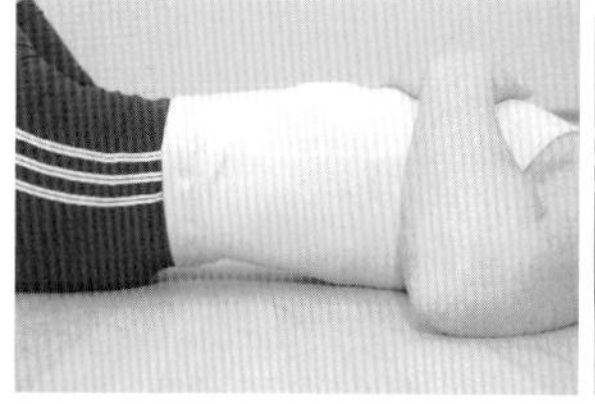

correct position

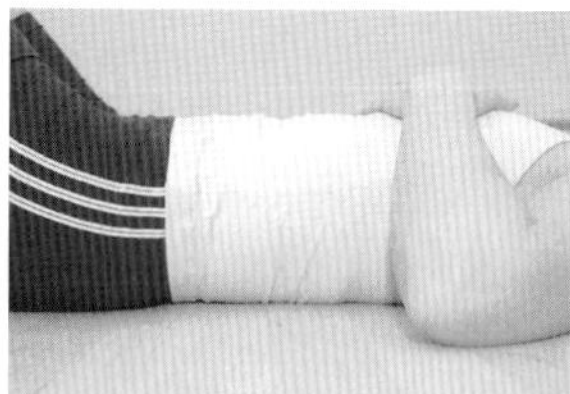

incorrect position

flat on the floor, under the small of your back.

Push your back down towards the floor and on to your hands.

Arch your back away from your hands (keeping your bottom on the floor) so that the small of your back is now clear of your hands.

Relax again, so that your back is lightly touching your fingers, then take your hands out from under your back.

If you can do this in front of a mirror, you will see a small space under your back. Focus on this position, as mentioned above, and remember it so that you can return to it at any time.

In the following tests you should retain strict neutral spine position – whether flat on the floor or elevated from it. It is common for the space in the small of your back to collapse the moment your stomach muscles are employed. This is a classic sign of weakness.

> *It matters not a jot if you can do a thousand traditional sit-ups – if you cannot carry out these tests while retaining control of your spine you are building a house of straw.*

The principles set out here are frequently seen in Pilates classes, and it can benefit anyone who is serious about their sport to invest some time checking out a class or two. You might think these classes look a bit namby-pamby, but once you try them you will understand just how eye-poppingly hard some of even the most subtle exercises are.

Exercises

Leg bridging: stage one

How to do it

Lie flat on your back with your knees bent and the soles of your feet on the floor. Place your arms across your chest and push down through the soles of both feet. Lift your backside clear of the floor – high enough to make a straight line between the shoulders, hips and knees. Hold for a count of three, with your spine in neutral position, and then slowly return to the starting position.

If you are not sure that you have achieved neutral spine position then try doing the exercise in front of a mirror. If you do not have a floor-level mirror at home or at the gym, then you will find that patio doors work a treat. If you have no problems after 10 repetitions, go to stage two of this exercise (see below).

Problems?

The most common problem is poor control through the movement (i.e. failing to achieve a consistent speed throughout the movement and 'falling' through the last few inches). Rectify this by resting your arms on the floor at your sides; this will allow your arms to assist you. Once your control has improved, go back to the arms-across-chest position.

Leg bridging: stage two

How to do it

As with stage one, lie flat on your back with your knees bent and the soles of your feet on the floor. Place your arms across your chest and push down through the soles of both feet. Lift your backside clear of the floor – high enough to form a straight line between the shoulders, hips and knees. Lift one foot off the floor. Keep your thighs parallel and

fully straighten the knee of the lifted leg. The aim of the exercise is to keep your trunk and hips steady throughout. Imagine that you have a brimful pint pot sitting on each hip and, as you lift your leg, you mustn't spill a drop.

Problems?

The most common problem is a dropping of the hip on the side of the raised leg. Another problem is an excessive sway of the trunk and hips towards the supporting leg. Rectify this by placing your arms on the floor at your sides as this will allow your arms to assist your balance. Once your control has improved, go back to the arms-across-chest position.

Abdominal curl

How to do it

Lie flat on a firm surface with your hands on your thighs in neutral spine position (see above). Sit up by curling your chin towards your chest, followed by your shoulder blades, then lifting your mid-back and finally your lower back from the floor. This must be done *slowly and smoothly*. Take at least four or five seconds to complete the movement.

Keep your heels in contact with the ground throughout. It is vital to keep the lowest part of the back in contact with the floor until the rest of the trunk has been raised from the floor. If this exercise feels easy, try doing it with your arms folded across your chest. Still easy? OK, then try it with your hands placed alongside your head (with your fingers outstretched and just touching your temples, not clasped behind your head or neck).

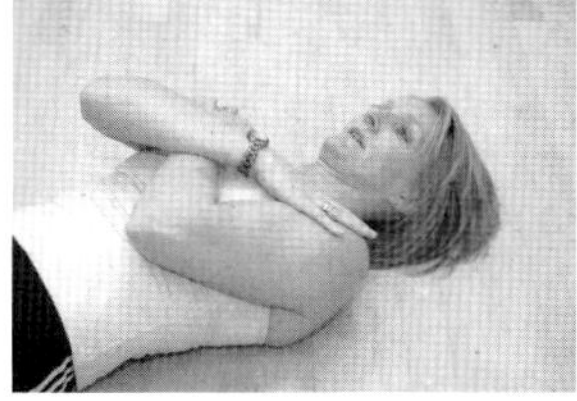

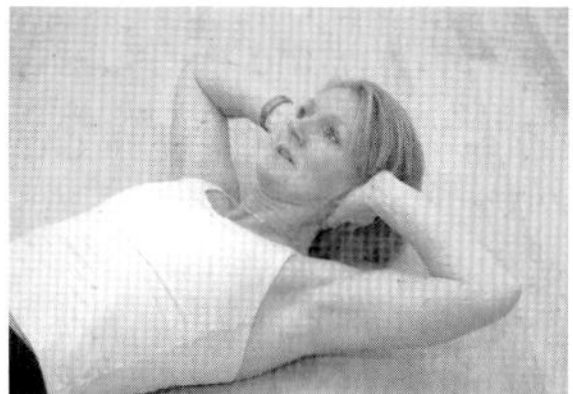

Problems?

The curled sit-up must be done smoothly. Any jerky movements indicate weakness or poor control. The early or mid parts of the curled sit-up are usually the places where difficulties arise. If you can't control the sit-up and do it smoothly and slowly, try the following. Start the sit-up from a semi-sitting position. This can be done by positioning your head, neck and shoulders against a wall, pillow or something similar. Practise the sit-up from this starting position and, as your control and strength improve, you can lower the starting point of the sit-up.

Back extension

How to do it

Lie flat on the floor, face down, with your hands by your sides. Brace your shoulders back and lift your head and shoulders clear of the floor. Do this slowly with good control.

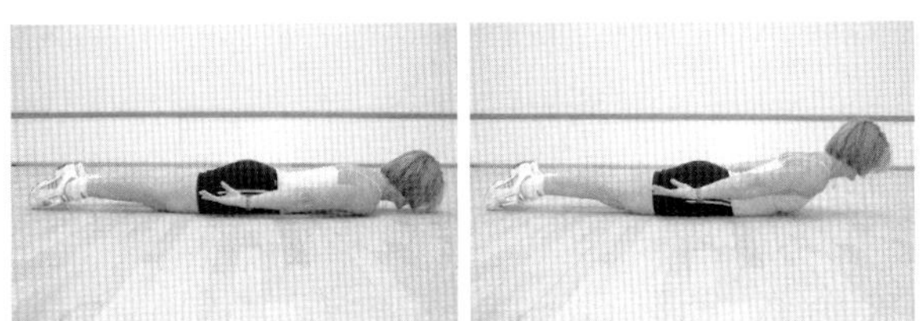

Problems?

Unable to clear your shoulders from the floor? This could be due to stiffness and/or weakness. If you can do a half press-up – that is, raise your shoulders off the floor using your hands (keeping your hips in contact with the floor) – then you have a weakness in your back muscles. If you can't, then the problem is one of stiffness. Doing half press-up exercises will help alleviate this.

Abductors (hips)

How to do it

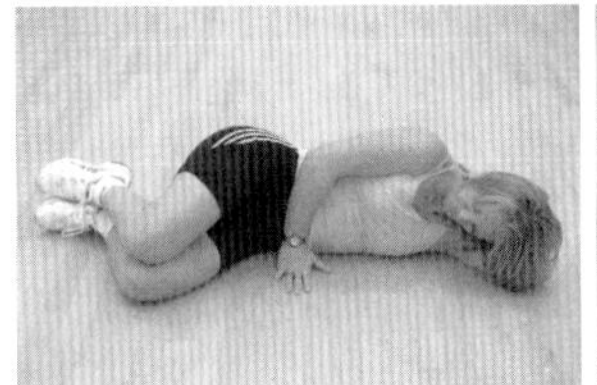

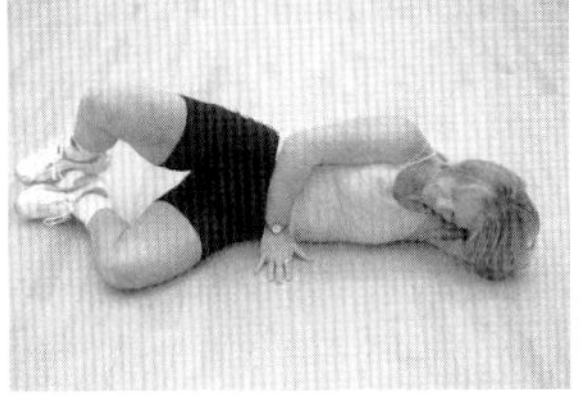

Lie on your side with both knees bent. Have your forearm and hand in front of your body to stop your trunk or hips from rolling forwards. Keeping your feet together, lift the top knee smoothly up towards the ceiling. **Do not** roll your trunk or hips forwards or backwards. If this is easy, use the same starting position then lift your top foot just clear of the bottom foot and repeat the same movement with your knee.

Problems?

If you are unable to lift the knee smoothly through the range, you can use this test as an exercise to improve the control of the abductors.

Adductors (groin)

How to do it

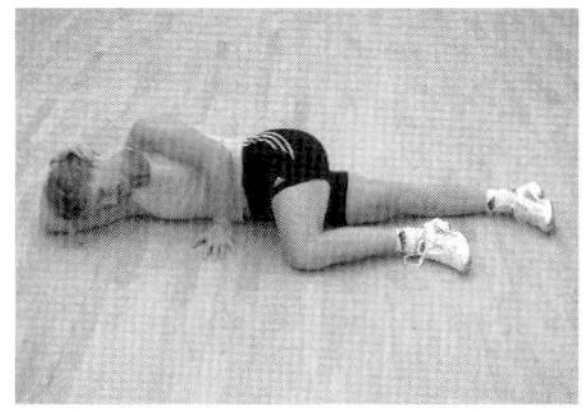

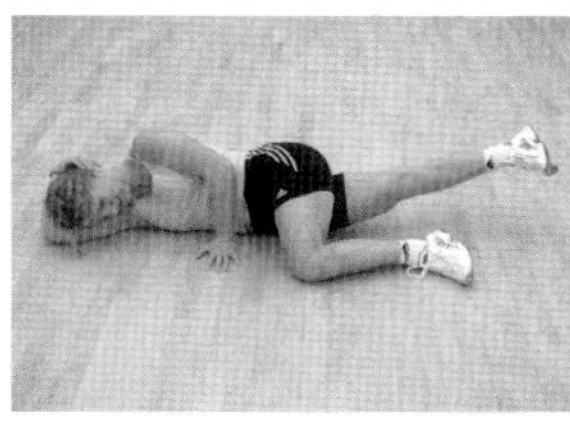

Lie on your side with your bottom leg straight and your top leg bent. Have your forearm and hand in front of your body to stop your trunk or hips from rolling forwards. Try to lift the bottom leg (leading with your heel), keeping your leg in line with your body and keeping the knee straight. The movement should be smooth and controlled and you should be able to lift the foot at least 6 inches from the floor.

Problems?

If you can't lift the leg at all or if you can only lift it up by bringing the leg forwards then the adductors are weak. This test can be used as an exercise to improve adductor control.

Initial testing and ongoing measurement

If you can't measure it, you can't manage it.

If you've got this far without any ill effects we can (we hope) safely assume that you are not a complete physical basket case. The next step is to look at ways in which you can measure your own performance now and as you develop and progress.

Our team of sports scientists puts professional athletes through such tests week in, week out. Usually, it takes us a week to complete a thorough assessment, but as you do not have the luxury of time, our years of experience have been compressed into a set of tests that you and your colleagues can complete in a matter of minutes. The results are just as robust and offer an excellent way to monitor progress and so help you stay motivated.

The key areas that we will now measure and assess are:

- explosive strength (also known as 'power')
- flexibility (how bendy you are)
- flat speed (your top speed)
- speed stamina (how long you can keep going at higher speed)
- cardiovascular capacity (how long you can keep going at lower intensity).

These tests have been selected and developed especially to tie in with the requirements of your sport, whose demands as you know are extremely varied. So it doesn't matter what your best bench press is or how much weight you can squat with – you are doing this to improve your rugby-playing ability. When asked what his bench press PB was, a GB champion shot putter was once heard to reply, '21 metres 15.' Similarly, the British Masters weightlifting champion, who can clean and jerk 160 kilos, was asked what he could bench press; he answered, 'Not sure, don't care.'

Get the point?

Don't mistake a means for an end, and remember those first two golden rules:

- pace yourself
- be honest.

It matters not a jot where you start with these tests – what we are seeking is *improvement* and *progression*. If you want to compare notes with a fellow training partner, then use 'percentage improvement' as your yardstick.

Test Quadrathlon

The first of our initial tests is called the 'Quadrathlon'.

The Quadrathlon was devised in 1982 to check the explosive power improvement of the Great Britain National Throws Squad; it is an internationally

'Once you stop working out, muscle will turn to fat ...'

Sorry – not a chance! Muscle and fat are two different tissues – muscle cannot turn to fat and fat cannot be converted into muscle. Instead, what happens is that when you stop training your muscles will gradually atrophy (get smaller) and ultimately return to their pre-trained size. This, in itself, can make you appear 'fatter'. Additionally, many people don't realise that increased muscle mass increases their metabolic rate; therefore a trained body will utilise more calories than an untrained one. However, once you stop training – unless you reassess your eating habits and take in fewer calories to account for your reduced muscle mass – you will gain body fat due to the excess calories you are consuming. These two factors generally combine to create the illusion of muscle turning to fat.

recognised test. The Quadrathlon is easy to carry out, and it offers an excellent way to test your fitness and progress. The test has four elements:

1. three jumps
2. standing long jump
3. 30-metre sprint
4. overhead shot throw.

It can be used to monitor your increases in power and, as it is a standardised test, you can use it to compare progress among your colleagues, providing a bit of friendly competition and so keeping things interesting. Record your times/ distances on a record sheet so that you can monitor your progress.

Important

Only carry out these tests on a reasonably soft surface – definitely not tarmac or concrete. If you ignore this advice, you and your knees, hips and back will be very sorry, very quickly. Grass is what you play on, so carry out the tests on a pitch.

How to perform the test

Three jumps

Start with your feet comfortably apart, with your toes just behind a take-off mark. Take three two-footed jumps, one immediately after the other. Keep your ankles together and bend your knees to cushion the joints as you jump. Simply measure the total distance you achieve. You must start with your feet still and you must land with your feet parallel at each jump phase. You can wear your boots if you like.

Standing long jump

Start exactly as for the previous test, but perform a single two-footed jump. Have a few goes and measure the longest distance you achieve. You should measure from the start line to the closest point of contact on landing (so if you fall backwards, mark where your backside/hand/ear touched the ground, not where your feet touched it).

30-metre sprint

This is a straight, eyeballs-out sprint. Ideally, you will need a partner to time you in order for this to be accurate. On the start signal, sprint from a stationary, standing set position to the finish line. Your partner should stand at the finish line and time you from when your first stride touches the ground to the moment your body crosses the line. Again, boots can be worn.

Overhead shot throw

Unless you have access to a 16 lb shot then it is DIY time. Lay your hands on a length of tyre inner tube, a bucket of sand and two heavy-duty cable ties (if you can't find cable ties then use strong wire). Cut a length from the tube about two feet long. Use one of the cable ties to tie off one end. Fill the tube with sand until it weighs 7.26 kg/16 lb (or 4 kg/8.8 lb for women), then tie off the other end with the other cable tie. Hey presto! A home-made medicine ball/shot.

If you are unable to do this, simply find a lump of something that weighs 16 pounds: a log or a breeze block cut down will do fine (they will just make a bit of a dent in the pitch when they land ...).

Stand on the touch line, with your back to pitch and with your feet a comfortable distance apart. The 'shot' should be held cupped in both hands.

Now crouch down, lowering the shot between your legs, then drive upwards to cast it back over your head. There is no penalty for following through (ahem), but you must land feet first and remain upright.

Measure from the outside of the touch line to the nearest point where the 'shot' touched the ground on landing.

Quadrathlon tables

Points are allocated from Quadrathlon tables (see Table 2.1 overleaf) depending on the distance or time achieved. Scores are compared with the athlete's previous scores to determine the level of improvement. Competition should be based on the improvement on the previous test for each event, *not* on absolutes.

Flat speed and speed endurance

The next phase of assessment considers your current position in relation to the following elements:

- acceleration
- base sprinting speed
- speed endurance (the ability to sustain top speed).

How to perform the test

Mark out a flat 120-metre straight. Split it into three with four markers: one at the start, one at 40 m, one at 80 m and one at 120 m.

From a standing set position, sprint flat out *through* the finishing line.

For accuracy, you will need a colleague to time you with three stopwatches, recording your times for 0–40 m, 40–80 m and 80–120 m. (You can get away with one watch if it has a lap timer and your assistant is not a muppet.) Essentially, you are performing a 40 m sprint followed by two consecutive 'flying 40s'.

What your times mean

Your 0–40 m time: It doesn't matter how quick this time is, it can always be improved upon. The importance of this phase will depend on your position – for instance, a scrum-half or no. 8 will have more need of this type of acceleration than a fullback, who will tend to sprint from a rolling start and will have more need of rapid pace change.

Your 40–80 m and 80–120 m times: If your times between these two flying 40s are identical, then you are in excellent shape to repeatedly sprint the short distances involved in rugby. If there is a variance of more than about 0.2 seconds, you will need to develop your speed stamina using the programmes described in later sections.

TABLE 2.1 Test Quadrathlon score table

Points	Three jumps	Standing long jump	30m sprint	Overhead shot	Points	Three jumps	Standing long jump	30m sprint	Overhead shot
1	3.00	1.00	5.80	4.00	51	7.04	2.36	4.38	12.58
2	3.08	1.02	5.77	4.17	52	7.12	2.39	4.35	12.75
3	3.16	1.05	5.74	4.34	53	7.19	2.41	4.33	12.92
4	3.24	1.08	5.71	4.51	54	7.28	2.44	4.30	13.10
5	3.32	1.10	5.68	4.68	55	7.36	2.47	4.27	13.27
6	3.40	1.13	5.66	4.85	56	7.44	2.50	4.24	13.44
7	3.48	1.16	5.63	5.03	57	7.52	2.52	4.21	13.61
8	3.56	1.19	5.60	5.20	58	7.60	2.55	4.18	13.78
9	3.64	1.21	5.57	5.37	59	7.68	2.58	4.16	13.95
10	3.72	1.24	5.54	5.54	60	7.76	2.60	4.13	14.13
11	3.80	1.27	5.51	5.71	61	7.84	2.63	4.10	14.3
12	3.88	1.30	5.49	5.88	62	7.92	2.66	4.07	14.47
13	3.96	1.32	5.46	6.06	63	8.01	2.69	4.04	14.64
14	4.05	1.35	5.43	6.23	64	8.09	2.71	4.02	14.81
15	4.13	1.38	5.40	6.40	65	8.17	2.74	3.99	14.98
16	4.21	1.40	5.37	6.57	66	8.25	2.77	3.96	15.16
17	4.29	1.43	5.34	6.74	67	8.33	2.80	3.93	15.33
18	4.37	1.46	5.32	6.91	68	8.41	2.82	3.90	15.50
19	4.45	1.49	5.29	7.09	69	8.49	2.85	3.87	15.67
20	4.53	1.51	5.26	7.26	70	8.57	2.88	3.85	15.84
21	4.61	1.54	5.23	7.43	71	8.65	2.90	3.82	16.02
22	4.69	1.57	5.20	7.60	72	8.73	2.93	3.79	16.19
23	4.77	1.60	5.17	7.77	73	8.81	2.96	3.76	16.36
24	4.85	1.62	5.15	7.94	74	8.89	2.99	3.73	16.53
25	4.93	1.65	5.12	8.12	75	8.97	3.01	3.70	16.70
26	5.02	1.68	5.09	8.29	76	9.06	3.04	3.68	16.87
27	5.10	1.70	5.06	8.46	77	9.14	3.07	3.65	17.12
28	5.18	1.73	5.03	8.63	78	9.22	3.10	3.62	17.29
29	5.26	1.76	5.01	8.80	79	9.30	3.12	3.59	17.46
30	5.34	1.79	4.98	8.97	80	9.38	3.15	3.56	17.63
31	5.42	1.81	4.95	9.15	81	9.46	3.18	3.53	17.80
32	5.50	1.84	4.92	9.32	82	9.54	3.20	3.51	17.97
33	5.58	1.87	4.89	9.49	83	9.62	3.23	3.48	18.06
34	5.66	1.90	4.86	9.66	84	9.70	3.26	3.45	18.23
35	5.74	1.92	4.84	9.83	85	9.78	3.29	3.42	18.42

TABLE 2.1 – continued

Points	Three jumps	Standing long jump	30m sprint	Overhead shot	Points	Three jumps	Standing long jump	30m sprint	Overhead shot
36	5.82	1.95	4.81	10.01	86	9.86	3.31	3.39	18.59
37	5.90	1.98	4.78	10.18	87	9.94	3.34	3.36	18.76
38	5.98	2.02	4.75	10.35	88	10.03	3.37	3.34	18.93
39	6.07	2.03	4.72	10.52	89	10.11	3.40	3.31	19.11
40	6.15	2.06	4.69	10.69	90	10.19	3.42	3.28	19.28
41	6.23	2.09	4.67	10.86	91	10.27	3.45	3.25	19.45
42	6.31	2.11	4.64	11.04	92	10.35	3.48	3.22	19.62
43	6.39	2.14	4.61	11.21	93	10.43	3.50	3.20	19.79
44	6.47	2.17	4.58	11.38	94	10.51	3.53	3.18	19.96
45	6.55	2.20	4.55	11.55	95	10.59	3.56	3.15	20.14
46	6.63	2.22	4.52	11.72	96	10.67	3.59	3.12	20.31
47	6.71	2.25	4.50	11.89	97	10.75	3.61	3.09	20.48
48	6.79	2.28	4.47	12.07	98	10.83	3.64	3.06	20.65
49	6.87	2.30	4.44	12.24	99	10.91	3.67	3.03	20.82
50	6.95	2.33	4.41	12.41	100	11.00	3.70	3.01	21.00

Measuring cardiovascular capacity

This is an area that can always be improved upon, and we will look in detail at improving and measuring your ability to keep going at low intensity for extended periods. On your progress sheet you need only record the duration of the exercise, which will increase week by week, as the intensity will remain constant.

The Harvard step test offers a good way to consistently gauge your level of cardiovascular (CV) capacity, and can be used in conjunction with the other tests described above (the Quadrathlon and 120 m sprint tests) to monitor your progress.

To undertake the Harvard step test you will need:

- a gym bench (45 cm high) – a beer crate is just as good
- a stopwatch
- an assistant.

The test is conducted by stepping up onto a standard gym bench once every two seconds until exhaustion, or for five minutes (150 steps) – whichever comes first. A single repetition is complete when both feet have returned to the start position. Note the following points.

- Have someone to help you keep to the required pace.
- One minute after finishing the test, take your pulse rate (beats per minute: bpm); record this as 'pulse A'.
- Two minutes after finishing the test, take your pulse rate (bpm); record this as 'pulse B'.
- Three minutes after finishing the test, take your pulse rate (bpm); record this as 'pulse C'.
- Scoring: the score is equal to (100 x test duration in seconds) divided by 2 x (total heartbeats in the recovery periods). Don't worry if this doesn't seem very clear to start with – use the ready reckoner below to do the necessary calculations which will determine your level of fitness.

1. Duration of exercise: ____ seconds x 100 = ____
    - Pulse A: ____ bpm
    - Pulse B: ____ bpm
    - Pulse C: ____ bpm
2. Add pulse counts A, B, C to get the total: ____ x 2 = ____
3. Divide the total of 1 by the total of 2 to get a total of ____

4. The total arrived at in 3 indicates a Harvard step test score of ____ (use the scale below to check what your score means).

   A score of:

   >90 = excellent

   80–89 = good

   65–79 = high average

   55–64 = low average

   <55 = poor.

Flexibility

To achieve your optimum level of speed, power and agility you must possess an adequate range of motion in, primarily, the shoulders, hips and ankles. Flexibility testing highlights areas of stiffness or tightness that can be worked on during your warm-down phase; this will reduce the chances of injury.

You can gauge your overall flexibility in under 10 minutes by carrying out the simple tests detailed below. If there are any of these tests that you can't do, concentrate on the weak area in question during your warm-*down* routine, not your warm-up (we will discuss this principle later).

None of the following tests provides any absolute measurements. They are valuable in that they offer a comparative measure that describes increases and improvements in flexibility.

Ankles

- Lie on your back with both legs extended and the backs of your heels on the floor.
- Point your toes as far away from you as possible – attempting to pass 45 degrees (i.e. halfway between the vertical and the floor).
- Compare the flexibility on each side.
- Now bring your toes back towards you as far as possible – attempting to pass the vertical the other way.
- Again, compare the flexibility on each side.

Elbows and wrists

- Spread out your fingers as wide as you can.
- Straighten your arm out in front of you, with the palm upwards. You should be able to rotate your palm so that your little finger is higher than your thumb.
- Don't bend your fingers; keep them outstretched at all times. We are measuring the flexibility of your forearm, not your fingers!
- Compare the flexibility on each side.

Groin

- While standing on one leg, raise the other leg out to the side.
- You are aiming to achieve an angle of 90 degrees between your legs.
- If you need to, you can hold on to something, or someone, to maintain balance.
- Ideally, stand with your back and heels against a wall. By keeping all your body in contact with the wall throughout, you will ensure that you don't cheat by leaning forwards or twisting your torso.
- Compare the flexibility on each side.

Hips

- Stand holding out a broomstick horizontally in front of you, one hand at each end, hands shoulder width apart.
- Without releasing your grip or moving your hands, bend down and step over the stick one leg at a time.
- Now step back through to return to the start position.
- Any acute inflexibility will mean you will not be able to complete this exercise.

Neck

- Normal flexibility will allow you to trap your flattened hand against your chest with your chin.

Shoulders

- In a standing position, attempt to clasp your hands behind your back by reaching behind your neck and downwards with one hand, and behind your back and upwards with the other.
- Try to link your fingers (or hands if you are more flexible).
- Repeat on the other side.
- Compare the flexibility on each side.

3 BUILDING ON SOLID GROUND
Best practice

aim:

- To give you an overview of the key exercises and drills that you will be using in your training schedules.

Warming up

Weak and brittle things break.

Contrary to traditional wisdom, a 'warm-up' is to prepare the body for exercise; it is not the best time to increase flexibility. Following exercise, the soft tissues will be warm and, as a result, their inherent ability to stretch will be increased. That's why attempts to increase basic flexibility should be made in the 'warm-down' period. For example, if you have one or two areas that you know are tight (hamstrings or calves, say), then it would be sensible to target these areas with stretches during your warm-down.

Be careful not to warm up for too long because you don't want to use up your energy warming up instead of saving it for an intense workout. You will need to sweat a little, but don't get fatigued by your warm-up. A good rule of thumb is to elevate your heart rate so that you are sweating lightly and are mildly out of breath. Five to seven minutes' light running is a good way of getting your body warmed up.

Essentially, a warm-up should mirror the exercises you are about to perform. There is no point in running for 10 minutes if you are planning to do a series of bench presses. Think about the range of movements you are preparing for and gradually build up the intensity to close to performance level. For example:

- **if you are in the gym**, perform one light set of each exercise and then gradually build up the weight
- **if you are on the track or on a field**, a steady jog for about two laps of a pitch/track followed by some low-intensity accelerations of about 2 x 100 m (jog into striding out, moving into three-quarter pace, then back to jog), followed by drills
- **before matches**, if your position involves scrummaging, quietly pack down with a team-mate and move each other *slowly* through a range of movement; *be sensible* – do not over-extend each other in this warm-up; if you are a three-quarter then warm up using the pitch/track routine above.

Alternatively, you can try skipping with a rope, which is a great all-over warm-up exercise. More on this later, but note that although skipping is an excellent way of warming up the whole body, it should be used as a precursor to, not a replacement for, an activity-specific warm-up.

top tip If you are going to skip, try to use a leather rope. It turns more quickly. New ones can be broken in quickly if you remove the leather, soak it for two days in water, dry it out and then leave it in olive oil overnight. While the oil is still wet, hammer along the length of the leather to break it in. Alternatively, you can use it for two years and it will reach the same supple state about a week before it wears out ...

Stretches

Try to hold each of the following stretches for 15–20 seconds.

Chest

Sit on the floor, legs stretched out in front of you. Rest your weight on your hands, which are resting on the floor behind your back. Keeping your hands where they are, and your arms straight, inch your bottom forwards. You should feel your chest and biceps stretch. If you do not, then return to the start position and move your hands closer together. Keep your chest puffed out and proud, to accentuate the stretch.

Triceps

Reach down behind your head with one arm, as far down your back as you can. With your free arm, *gently* push down on the elbow to increase the stretch. Keep your back and neck straight.

Back (upper)

Sit cross-legged on the floor. Reach forwards with both arms as far as you can. Relax your neck and keep your head up throughout the stretch. You will feel the centre of your upper back begin to stretch. Hold, and then reach over to your left as far as you can with your right hand; hold again, then repeat on the other side.

Back (lower)

Lie flat on your back with your arms outstretched to each side, in a crucifix position. Bring your right knee up towards your chest and roll it over to your left side, keeping your upper body still and your back still flat(tish) on the floor. Hold, and then change sides.

Abs

Lie face down on the floor in a press-up position. Keeping your hips in contact with the floor at all times, press up, arching your back. Leaning your head back, look up as high as you can. You will feel your stomach muscles stretch. Push down with your hips to accentuate the stretch. To isolate the obliques (the muscles down the sides of the stomach) repeat as before, but look up and right as far as you can, then repeat looking to the left.

Neck

Sitting or standing upright, look over to your right as far as you can; try to put your chin on your shoulder. Slowly follow a semi-circular path down past your chest and up to the left, stretching all the time. Try to put your left ear on your left shoulder. Hold, then change sides.

There are many other excellent stretching routines, but the above offer a good basis from which to start. If you find other stretches that work for you then add them to your routine.

If you are about to do speed work of any kind (including ball work at club training), then you should also include the following warm-ups.

Accelerations

Mark out 100 m into (roughly) 4 x 25 m sections. Starting at a dead jog, slowly build up at every 25 m marker until you reach seven-eighths' pace for the last section. *Walk* back slowly and repeat, building up to five times.

Bounding

Exaggerate the perfect running motion. Concentrate on driving back with your elbows and up with your knees to ensure maximum range of movement. You are

'Weight training makes you muscle-bound ...'

This is an old chestnut that is losing credibility by the day, thank goodness. 'Muscle-bound-ness' has never been satisfactorily defined, but if it means poor performance due to inflexibility or lack of co-ordination then there is simply no evidence for it. Almost all serious athletes (whatever their sport) include weight training as an integral part of their preparation. However, bearing in mind that 'practice makes permanent', lots of slow, heavy exercises will not, on their own, produce a fast, powerful, dynamic rugby player. Common sense?

attempting to explode off the track/field with every stride and 'hang' for as long as possible. Compete with yourself: how far can you travel with 10 bounds? Remember that your initial result is not too important, but your improvement *is*! Start by doing about 2 x 20 m and work up to 6 x 40 m as you perfect the action.

Strength training

Bearing in mind that, just as brittle things break, so do those that are weak, strength training is going to be an important part of a rugby player's repertoire. The overall aims of strength training are to improve a combination of performance and appearance.

Don't be shy about the importance of appearance – as long as it is viewed only as a by-product and not a goal to the exclusion of strength. It will make you feel better about yourself and you are likely to find that you will reach a stage when training is important to you because you like how you are starting to look and feel. Again it's that word honesty – we are all vain buggers. (But don't kid yourself that you are going to have a washboard stomach without living like a monk. Be realistic about your objectives.)

As mentioned in earlier chapters, *planned progression is everything*. Hold that thought and not only will it keep you safe, it will keep you motivated too. This principle is particularly important when it comes to strength training. It does not matter what you can lift, it only matters that you become stronger than you are now, and thus improve your game, avoid injury and get progressively more satisfaction from the sport.

top tip Whatever else you do or don't do, remember to *keep a training diary*; record distance runs, sprints, every detail of your strength conditioning, games, your stretching and everything else. This will give you more motivation than a thousand psychologists! Be honest, accurate, detailed and up to date. If it isn't written down, it didn't happen!

The rational for compound exercises

Figure 1

Figure 2

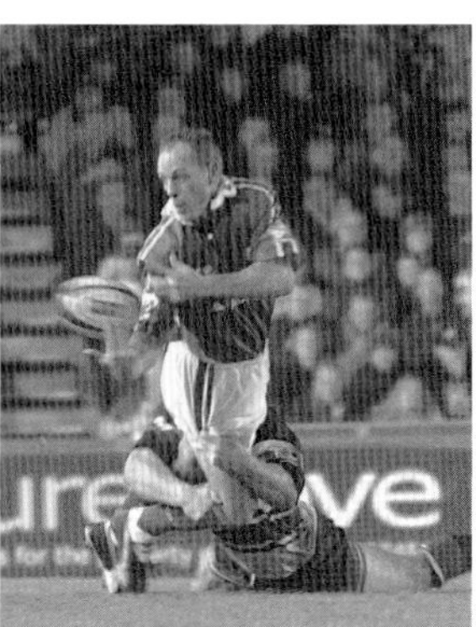
Figure 3

This series of photographs illustrates precisely why resistance training for Rugby should favour compound over simple (or isolation) exercises.

In figure 1 John Holtby and Harry Ellis scrag a London Irish attacker. Holtby (left) attempts to turn the player and is using his shoulder, legs, arms, back and stomach muscles in a twisting motion. This movement is delivered by a combination of all these joints and muscles.

So it can be seen that in training a Cheat One Hand Row is much more appropriate than (for example) a bicep curl as the C1H Row recruits back, arm, shoulder, stomach and even leg muscles.

In just the same way Graham Rowntree demonstrates (figure 2) the complexity of pushing movements in a game. The effort he is delivering is unevenly distributed and incorporates his whole body. So again we see that isolation exercises bear little resemblance to the demands of the game. A relevant exercise would be a one hand snatch that requires coordination, explosive power, stability and strength.

. . . and if you wanted proof positive of the importance of a strong 'core' see figure 3. Glenn Gelderbloom delivers a pass out of a tackle which, having wrapped up his legs, leaves only his upper body free to generate the movements required for the pass.

The rotational work in training that combines all sections of the trunk and incorporates complex twisting motions with resistance ensures that when you need to generate power like this you are not left wanting.

A glossary of terms

Before we go any further, let us define some of the terms you will encounter that you may not have come across before. There will be others, but we'll explain those as we go along.

- **Aerobic exercise** – exercise in which muscles' demand for oxygen equals the body's ability to supply it.
- **Anaerobic exercise** – exercise in which muscles' demand for oxygen exceeds the body's ability to supply it; it produces quantities of lactic acid (the 'burn' you feel when a muscle exhausts).
- **Ballistic movement** – when the inertia of the weight takes over. Not good. Often encountered because the movement is too fast and uncontrolled. The official description is: 'A fast, large-range movement that uses the momentum of a body part to exert an end-of-range stretch. Due to the speed and large amplitude of movement, this type of stretch is difficult to control and could cause injury.'
- **Compound exercise** – an exercise that employs a number of different muscles at once (e.g. bench press = chest and triceps).
- **Concentric** – the positive action when the muscle shortens under resistance (e.g. the up phase of a bench press).
- **Eccentric** – the negative phase when the muscle lengthens under resistance (e.g. the down phase of a bench press).
- **Muscle fibres (fast-twitch and slow-twitch)** – muscles are made up of different types of fibre. Fast-twitch fibres are for short, explosive work, slow-twitch fibres for more sustained levels of effort at lower intensity. You are born with a certain proportion of both and can't change this totally, but you can develop what you have.
- **'Prime mover' exercise** – the opposite of a compound exercise; one that isolates one muscle group at a time (e.g. bicep curl).

- **Static or isometric** – when a muscle is under resistance but not moving (i.e. muscle contraction with no appreciable change in length). The classic example is to stand in a doorway and push out to the sides against the door frame with both hands. (Unless your name is Hercules or Samson, you are unlikely to move anything!)

Basic training principles

Remember, we are looking for weight training that mirrors what you do on the field. We want strength combined with speed. To achieve this, you must be strict about your form during exercise. Be slow and controlled through the eccentric phase and then power up through the concentric phase. Exercising in this way means that all the muscle fibres (both slow-twitch and fast-twitch) are employed.

Let's take bench presses as an example: down slowly (count one, two, three); halt the bar just as it is lightly touching your nipples, but so the weight is still in your hands; hold for a moment and then bang the bar up hard and fast. Lock out at the top before you start again.

Moving the weight too fast is known as ballistic movement, and this is not good for a number of reasons:

- Lack of control means that the movement can be taken too far and injuries sustained.
- The muscle is not under resistance through its full range. Imagine this a bit like a child's swing: if you had to push it through its full range slowly, this would require effort all the way up and down; if you push it fast, you can stand still and simply give it a shove now and again to maintain the momentum.

Which weight?

Remember golden rule 2 – pace yourself. There are no absolutes and it's only improvement that matters. So be honest with yourself and use the correct weight for what you are doing. Of course, it should not be too light, but it definitely shouldn't be too heavy either. Don't be tempted to show off by 'going ballistic'. It is always more impressive to see someone who knows what they are doing rather than some idiot who thinks that the gym is the place for some sort of masculinity contest. Training in the gym should be done in a competitive atmosphere, but the competition is with yourself and your own development, not with the jerk in the flashy singlet (you can usually identify this guy by the fact that he has phantom lats and pretends his muscles are so huge that his arms cannot hang properly by his sides ... yeah right).

You will be surprised at the lack of weight needed to overload a muscle if you are *really* strict. (That sounds a bit like golden rule 3: quality before quantity – always!)

Order of play

When working out, it is best to train the larger muscles first and smaller muscles last. Training large muscle groups (thighs, chest and back) will take the majority of your energy; that's why you need to train these large muscle groups when you are at your strongest.

Smaller muscles (biceps, triceps and forearms) should be trained after the larger muscles because it doesn't take as much energy to train them. If you train the smaller muscles first then you will not have enough strength left to train your larger muscles. Also, try to start with compound exercises and work your way up to simple routines.

To sum up, if you train your biceps first, you will not have enough strength in your arms to train your back muscles, for example. And you should try to order your workout so that you alternate 'push' exercises (e.g. dips) with 'pull' exercises (e.g. upright rows).

Spotting

If you are going to use free weights, it will be difficult to ensure a really intense and safe programme unless you use a 'spotter' (someone who assists you in the ways listed below). If you train with a spotter or have been asked by a stranger at the gym to act as their spotter, there are some simple guidelines you should follow. It's a big responsibility for either party. Choose your spotter wisely and make sure that, if you are doing the spotting, you do so to the very best of your abilities.

- Pay attention to the person you are spotting at all times. Don't look at the totty/trouser across the room doing deep knee bends.
- Be prepared, instantly, to help the person you are spotting.

- Ask the person you are spotting if they would like you to put your hands on the bar/weights (some people like this and some don't).
- Ask the person you are spotting how many reps they think they can handle on their own.
- Make sure that you can handle the weight that the person you are spotting is using. If you don't think you can handle it, don't be macho and try to 'help' anyway.
- Offer only the effort the person you are spotting requires from you. Don't let the weight jerk around while they are trying to lift it, but *never* assist the last rep, and tell your spotter not to assist you. Make every rep an *honest* rep.
- Offer encouragement to the person you are spotting. This will really help them. With your encouragement, they might find they can squeeze out those last few reps.

How many reps should you be doing?

Deciding on the amount of repetitions you do depends on what you are trying to accomplish, but golden rule 3 always applies: quality before quantity – always! No more repetitions than can be performed with perfect form.

If you want to gain mass

Don't become too obsessed with growth, as you are the one who has to move all that extra weight around the park. However, the principle here is heavy weights, few reps per set.

For body mass – if you can perform 16 reps, the weight you are using is too light. If you can't do eight, it's too heavy. Start at what you can manage about 10 times and build up to 16, then increase the weight, drop the reps and build up to 16 again.

For strength with much less weight gain – start at what you can do six, but not 10, times. Build up to 10 reps and then add weight.

Remember, when we get to the phases described in the next chapter, in phase one you will do many exercises but only one set of each. You should rest for about two minutes between each set/exercise (and keep this consistent so that you know you are not wasting time).

myth buster

'You need to eat loads of protein to gain muscle mass ...'

Although you do need enough protein in order to build muscle mass, excess protein intake will not result in enhanced muscle growth. It is true that training of any kind increases protein needs, but there is no scientific evidence to suggest that any athlete needs more than 1.8 kg of protein per day. In fact, the excess dietary protein that many strength-trained athletes consume isn't funnelled directly into muscle growth – it is more likely to be converted into carbohydrate, which is then metabolised for energy. So, it makes more sense to consume it as carbohydrate in the first place.

This goes against the received 'wisdom' presented in many so-called fitness magazines, which are owned or supported by advertising revenue from ... er ... sports supplement producers. Hmm.

Rest

Most people lead very hectic lives and they don't get the rest or sleep they need. If you are training hard, you need to rest in order to recharge your batteries. You can't be at peak efficiency by staying up until one in the morning and getting up at six o'clock the next morning for days on end.

There was an article in a 1970 copy of *Ironman* magazine written by Arthur Jones, the creator of Nautilus workout machines. The article stated that

Arthur Jones could add one to two inches to any highly motivated bodybuilder. He basically took some of these bodybuilders in and told them to sleep and rest for the next three nights and days. After this time, most of the bodybuilders had already gained quarter of an inch on their arms.

Of course, we are not looking for ornamental muscle here, but the principle is sound. Over-training is not the preserve of elite athletes. The broad rules are:

- get 10 hours of sleep per night if you are a teenager
- get eight to nine hours of sleep per night if you are an adult
- schedule a 15-minute nap in the middle of the afternoon (most people can't do this, but if you are lucky enough to get the opportunity take it)
- keep vigorous activity to a minimum on your days off
- take a week off after six months of steady training.

Most of you will have to balance the demands of work, home, sport, family and so on, and will have to find a happy medium, but don't underestimate the importance of rest. In the right proportion it is as important as time in the gym or on the training field.

Rest while you are working out is an important factor to monitor for two reasons. First, if you time your rest between sets and between exercises then you can slowly reduce it and so increase the intensity. Second, by keeping tabs on your rest periods you can keep your session moving along nicely. Here's an example: aim to work up to 30 seconds between sets and 60 seconds between exercises; by doing this, you can keep your workout under an hour.

When you work with time restrictions you work more effectively and are less likely to slip into the sloppy mindset that can take over when there is no deadline.

Machines versus free weights

Are free weights better than machines? Well, it depends who you talk to. There is an argument to say that free weights offer a better simulation of real-life demands on your muscles; this is because the instability they provide recruits many stabilising muscles that don't operate during machine workouts. Anyway, here are the pros and cons so you can make up your own mind.

The advantages of machines

- They are great for beginners because they are safe and easy to use.
- Machines guide your body through a specific range of movement.
- You don't have to worry about balancing the weight as much as with free weights.
- Machines don't require as much co-ordination.
- Machines isolate each muscle group.
- Machines are usually arranged in sequence so that you work large muscle groups and then smaller muscle groups.

The disadvantages of machines

- Machines don't fit everybody. They can be hard to adjust.
- Machines don't build as much balance or co-ordination.
- Machines can force your body into an uncomfortable range of movement. (If you feel uncomfortable, move on to another machine.)
- Machines are not portable. They can't be moved around very easily.
- Many trainers believe that working out with machines alone doesn't produce very effective results.

The advantages of free weights

- Free weights are versatile. One set of dumbbells can be used for many exercises.
- Free weights build better balance and co-ordination.
- Free weights work your muscles in a way that matches real-life demands.
- Free weights allow you to strengthen muscles and tendons that wouldn't get much work if you were using machines (i.e. the smaller, stabilising muscles).

The disadvantages of free weights

- Free weights can be difficult because of the balance and co-ordination required. (But then who said anything worthwhile was easy?)

Basic technique in the gym

This section describes the core principles of gym work and how the key exercises should be performed. No doubt you have been working out for years and know it all. You may well do, but everyone can benefit from a coach reviewing form from time to time. Over time you can slip into bad habits so take this as an opportunity to go back to basics and check out your technique.

Each of the following exercises is looking for a basic technique, which should be strictly observed for every rep. Many bodybuilders will say 'the slower the better'; that's fine for the beach, but bear in mind that we are looking for the development of explosive power. (The exact nature of the exercise most suited to your own position will be discussed later.)

For example, in order to develop power, the bench press would be performed in a 1–4 sequence, as follows.

1. Slowly through the eccentric phase.

   (Bar comes down slowly to lightly touch the chest, for a count of three.)

2. Pause at the 'bottom' of the exercise, just long enough to halt the bar.

   (*Don't go 'ballistic'.*)

3. Fast through the concentric phase.

   (*Bar driven up quickly and elbows locked out.*)

4. Pause at the 'top' of the exercise, again just long enough to halt the bar.

Note that, although some exercises follow this 1–4 pattern (e.g. bench press), some will start with the concentric phase. For example, the two-hand curl starts with the bar resting against the thighs with elbows locked out (at the 'bottom' of the exercise). Keeping the elbows against the sides at all times and the back straight, it runs through the following sequence of movements.

3. Fast through the concentric phase.

   (*Bar comes up to touch the chest.*)

4. Pause bar at the 'top' of the exercise.

1. Slowly through the eccentric phase.

   (*Bar returns slowly to start and elbows lock out.*)

2. Pause at the 'bottom' of the exercise, again just long enough to halt the bar.

   (*Don't go 'ballistic'.*)

Breathing

With almost all exercises it is important to breathe out during the concentric phase and in on the eccentric.

> *Remember, the quality of the exercise, and therefore what you will get out of it, depends on retaining consistent, top-quality form throughout all exercises and all reps. One last poor-quality rep shouldn't – and mustn't – count.*

Keep your form!

Weight belts and straps

The basic principle is that no one plays rugby with a weight belt on ...

Many people work out with their weight belts permanently fastened. It's up to you, but all that is doing is ensuring that your lower back is not properly employed. This can easily lead to a weak back that needs protecting, and in this way, a vicious circle is set up. (Why people wear them to do biceps curls is a mystery! Maybe they think kit = proficiency. And please don't ever carry a weight belt on the outside of your kit bag outside a gym; there is a certain code, you know ...)

If someone says, 'I've got a weak back so I have to protect it', the answer is 'Lose the belt, reduce the weight and sort out your technique.' If your back, knees, or whatever, are not up to the controlled stresses of the gym then they are certainly not up to the rigours of rugby.

However, if you are doing a heavy lifts session (see later sections), once in a while wearing a weight belt is a sensible precaution. Other than that, the benefits are questionable. In the end it's up to you, though.

By the same token, try to limit the use of lifting wrist straps to exercises where you are limiting the stress that can be applied to a muscle group to the amount of strain the forearms can take. A good example is pull-ups where, on a final set, your back may still be going strong but you have exhausted your grip. At this point use straps to get that last set out. If you are going to use them, do so sparingly because (just as with belts) over-use will lead to weakness.

Core exercises

What follows is a description of all the key exercises and how they should be performed. There are, literally, hundreds of different lifts with which any gym rat will bore you endlessly. Remember that we are looking for maximum effect for time invested. With this in mind, limit the exercises to those that provide the best overall returns. These are 'compound exercises' that employ more than one muscle at a time and, apart from being more time-effective, they replicate the demands of the game more closely.

The first set are the core exercises you will employ. You will notice that they deal with pushing and pulling in all three planes: overhead, in front and downwards. Pay particular attention to how they should be performed as this will be very different from the slow, laborious way a bodybuilder would train. (Remember, 'train slow, play slow'.)

We will deal with the number of reps you need to do in a later section.

The exercises and programmes in this book are intended as a guide only and you should try to get a qualified coach to check you out on a reasonably regular basis.

Keep your form

At all times use a weight that will allow you to perform each exercise strictly, and then progress gradually to heavier weights. You will notice that, because of the importance placed on the abdomen, the exercises that target and strengthen this area are dealt with separately in each of the three phases described in Chapter 4.

Alternate dumbbell press

Muscles employed: Shoulders, upper chest

Start position

Sitting, knees and ankles together, dumbbells resting on shoulders

How to do it

Drive dumbbells, one at a time, vertically

Try to ensure that the weights go straight up and down. Don't wander off at an angle. At the top of the movement, your elbow should be locked, with the weight directly above the shoulder. Lower steadily and repeat with the other arm. By sitting and keeping your knees together, your shoulders will be isolated more acutely. Keep your back straight – don't rock back and forth. If you do, then lose some of the weight.

Pull-up (long arm)

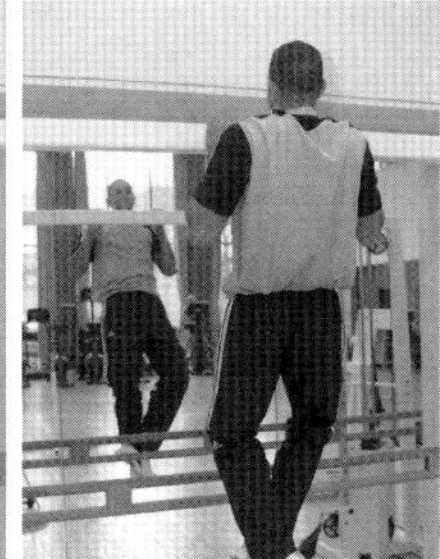

Muscles employed: Back, biceps

Start position

On a chin-up bar, grasp the bar with your palms facing **away from you**, hands slightly more than shoulder width apart; hang so that your arms are locked out

How to do it

Pull yourself up so that your chin is above the bar, hold and then slowly return to the start position

Ensure that you lock out under control at the bottom of the exercise and don't 'bounce'. Try to keep your knees pointing at the ground and your feet up behind you as this more accurately targets the back muscles. You will not be able to do too many of these, so on the last rep give yourself a boost up and lower as slowly as possible – this negative rep will eventually help you to achieve more full reps.

Bench press

Muscles employed: Chest, triceps

Start position
Hands shoulder width apart on the bar (or holding dumbbells if you prefer); elbows locked out

How to do it
Steadily and keeping it under control, lower the bar to the chest; pause and then drive back up

The wider the grip, the more the chest is isolated. A narrower grip will isolate the triceps. This exercise can be performed with a barbell or dumbbells. *Always use a spotter for this exercise.*

Cheat one-hand row

(Note that this exercise is not to be confused with the 'one-hand row' that body-builders use to target triceps.)

Muscles employed: Back (lats, rhomboids), biceps, back of the shoulder (posterior deltoids)

Start position
Lean on a bench with your right hand so that your torso is parallel with the floor and your feet are about shoulder

width apart. Reach down with your left hand to pick up a dumbbell from in front of your right foot. The perfect position is with your spine in line with the bench, not angling off to one side.

How to do it

In one clean movement bring the weight straight up so that it is touching your chest between your nipple and your armpit

Follow the movement through by rotating your back, and try to look up and behind you to ensure good rotation. Return the weight to the start position. It's a good idea to imagine that your spine is a hinge and the body is rotating around it; in this way you are using only the targeted muscles to move and control the weight. Ensure that the bench is high enough to require you to reach right down for the weight. This provides a rotational movement of the back muscles at the bottom and the top of the exercise.

Dips

Muscles employed: Triceps, lower chest

Start position

In a parallel dip rack, start with your arms at full extension

How to do it

Bend your arms slowly until your shoulders are as close to your hands as possible; pause, and then drive up hard to return to the start position

You can add weight by hanging weight discs from a belt with a chain looped through it. If you haven't got a dip rack then most squat/bench racks have handles on them for this exercise (see the illustrations). An alternative is to set up two benches in parallel; start with your feet up on one and your hands on the other, just behind your hips. Proceed as above. More weight can be added by resting weights in your lap.

Upright row

Muscles employed: Back (lats, rhomboids), biceps, backs of shoulders (anterior deltoids)

Start position

Stand (back straight, looking straight ahead) holding a barbell, which should be touching your hips, your arms locked out and legs slightly bent to reduce any strain on the lower back; your hands should be close together on the bar (about two thumb lengths apart)

How to do it

Pull the bar up to your chin, keeping your elbows as high as possible; pause at the top and then lower slowly to the start position

Do not drop the bar through the last few inches as this is a great way to damage your shoulders and back. Keep the bar under control at all times.

Side bends

Muscles employed: Back (lats), sides (obliques), abdominal muscles

Start position

Back straight, feet slightly wider than shoulder width apart, holding a dumbbell in your left hand against the outside of your left leg; your right hand should be against the side of your head

How to do it

Lower the dumbbell down the line of your left leg as far as it will go; pause, and then bring it back to the start. Concentrate on keeping your right elbow from coming forward as you dip sideways; this will ensure that you are tipping sideways rather than forwards, correctly isolating the muscles at the side of your trunk.

This is a subtle exercise, so strive for correct form at all times. Repeat holding the dumbbell in your right hand.

Ensure that you do not lean forwards during the exercise as this transfers any stress to your back. A good tip is to watch the weights at all times.

Sides and fronts

Muscles employed: Shoulders (deltoids), upper back/neck (trapezius) and upper chest

Start position
Stand up straight, shoulders square, with a light dumbbell in each hand; keep your upper body still and your arms straight at all times; bend your knees slightly to take the strain off your lower back

How to do it
Part 1: starting with the dumbbells resting on the front of your thighs, palms facing each other, raise the weights to the front until your arms are parallel with the floor; return to the start; at the top of the exercise, ensure that your thumbs are pointing dead ahead as this places more emphasis on the upper chest and the front of the shoulders

Part 2: starting again with the dumbbells resting on the front of your thighs, palms facing each other, raise the weights out to the side, in line with your body, so that your arms are parallel to the floor; at the top of the exercise ensure that your thumbs are pointing straight down. This places stress on the rear of the shoulder (the deltoids)

Return to the start and repeat Part 1 followed by Part 2, and so on.

Screw curls

Muscles employed: The front of the arm and the front of the shoulder

Start position

As for the standard bicep curl, except that you keep the dumbbell in parallel with your body (i.e. your palm facing inwards)

How to do it

Perform a curl as described earlier, but finish with your palm facing your chest so that the dumbbell twists through 90 degrees from start to finish

Lower body strength training

There is always a temptation to omit squats from training routines. There is a reason for this. There is a tendency for people to perform these exercises badly, which then puts massive strain on the knees and back – not good. Also, it tends to be a very slow exercise, which does nothing for the dynamic power a rugby player needs. (Later on, you will see some schedules that feature Olympic lifts, which offer a much more dynamic leg workout than squats alone.) However, if performed accurately and starting with a low weight to perfect technique, squats can add great value to your training.

Safety considerations for the squat

Keep your chest high, head up and back flat throughout. Use manageable loads until your technique is perfect and *ingrained*! Use spotters (see pictures opposite) or a squat rack; *never* squat down on to a bench – one heavy sit-down and you'll have destroyed your vertebral discs! Use either full or half squats in a session, not both. You may use light

jump squats after either full or half squats for a very dynamic, demanding workout for the legs.

Full squat

CORE-VITAL EXERCISE FOR FORWARDS

Targets the hip and leg extensors, and all trunk muscles used to maintain correct posture.

Face the squat rack, on which the bar should be at just below shoulder height. Take the bar on your shoulders, stand up and take a step back. Keep your feet flat on the floor, just over hip width apart, toes pointing slightly outwards.

Breathe in and bend your knees until your thighs are parallel to the ground. Keep your back flat and vertical; hold for a moment, then, breathing out, powerfully straighten your legs and push your hips forwards until you are upright. *Do not 'snap' your knees back at the top of this exercise as this can over-extend the joint and cause injury.*

Half squat

CORE-VITAL EXERCISE FOR BACKS

Proceed as for the full squat but only bend your knees until your thighs are at an angle of 45 degrees to the floor; hold, then drive strongly back to full upright position. Inhale while lowering, exhale while driving upwards.

Jump squat (or vertical jump)

CORE-VITAL EXERCISE FOR EVERYONE – VITAL FOR THE DEVELOPMENT OF EXPLOSIVE POWER

Follow the starting and safety procedures as for the full squat but there should be less of a knee-bend and much less weight used than in the half squat. When in your lowest position (as shown in the accompanying photograph) jump vertically upwards and, on landing, *rebound*. Keep your back flat, your head up and your body vertical. Note that you should keep your knees bent to cushion your landing.

The stages to be followed are:

1. **start** – descend to a half-squat position
2. **jump** – drive powerfully upwards to just clear the floor (an inch will do)
3. **receive** – land and halt the movement with your knees bent to cushion your landing, in much the same way that a cricketer will catch a ball with 'soft' hands; essentially, you are now back to the start position
4. **recover** – stand up.

The exercise is performed as follows:

start → jump → receive/jump/receive → hold for two seconds and then recover = one repetition

IMPORTANT

For safety it is vital that you start with very light weights and build slowly with this exercise. Struggling with heavy weights will lead directly to poor form and execution, and almost certainly injury.

Olympic lifting technique

Why lifts?

Olympic lifts use more muscle groups and more muscle mass in complex movement than any other movement or exercise – and they use them *fast*, unlike power lifting (bench presses, squats and dead lifts). This means that you train speed, co-ordination and explosive strength, right from the early stages. Look at the photos in this section and see for yourself!

Simple precautions

You will need sturdy supportive footwear, not beat-up old trainers! You will also need an uncluttered area for lifting, with a non-slip floor. Use Olympic (20 kg) bars whenever possible – they have revolving sleeves and allow the hands to flip or rotate without the mass of the discs causing the bar to twist, which might result in breaking your grip or damaging your wrists.

Each exercise is accompanied by illustrations to help demonstrate the basics of the techniques required. Start off with light weights and concentrate on technique, building up gradually. Because form and technique are so vital, it is a good idea to train with a partner so you can check each other out as you go. If you have an experienced lifter at your gym who can review your lifts periodically, so much the better.

Old lifters' maxim: 'Start small – finish tall. Arms last and very fast!'

You are strongly advised not to max out on any of these lifts without proper tuition, supervision and practice. You will get plenty of benefit from using lighter weights and strict form on each rep.

top tip Olympic weights are all nine inches in radius because this is a safe height from which to begin lifts. Starting any lower (i.e. with smaller-diameter discs) would put unnecessary strain on your back and knees. Most gymnasiums only have nine-inch-radius weights, starting at 20 kg, including a bar (an Olympic bar is 20 kg) that is a minimum of 60 kg – a bit too heavy for practising complex lifts. You can get round this problem by building some wooden dummy weights. Cut two nine-inch-radius discs out of plywood or MDF and put holes in the centre to fit your barbell. This means that you can practise the movements in safety – without any weights at all, perhaps – and build up gradually by adding small weights to the dummies. You can do the same with one-inch-diameter bars.

One-hand power snatch

Whilst not strictly an Olympic lift, this is the safest, most dynamic, most important and most relevant lift of all; the one-hand snatch will strengthen quadriceps, hip extensors, lower back, hamstrings and backside, calf muscles, upper back, shoulders, back, biceps, chest and triceps – and give a great plyometric workout to the whole body as the dumbbell is 'caught' overhead. It is an exercise where, even if technique is not perfect, maximum effort can be made.

It will also greatly improve trunk (core) stability, as one side of the body works while the other stabilises. There are few human movements where the muscular effort is equal on both sides of the body – you run left, right, left, right; punch and kick with one limb at a time – so the one-hand snatch is an excellent training exercise.

Note that the path of the dumbbell is near vertical throughout this lift.

GET SET

Start with your feet just over hip width apart. Your back should be flat and your shoulders just over the weight. The dumbbell should be on the floor parallel to your shoulders and between your feet; one hand should over-grip the dumbbell with your knuckles facing forwards. Keep your head up, looking forwards. Keep your lifting arm relaxed but with some pull on the dumbbell (so that there is no slack that will allow you to 'jerk' and jar your shoulder muscles). Your free hand should rest on your thigh, just above knee.

FIRST PULL

Ease the weight off the floor (no jerking!) by driving through your heels and, as the weight passes your shins, push down hard on your thigh with your free hand to give extra acceleration. Keep your lifting arm straight, and keep accelerating the dumbbell. When the dumbbell is level with your groin, move on to the ...

SECOND PULL

Keep accelerating the weight, rise on to your toes, raise (shrug) your shoulder and fully extend your body. (The weight should be moving at its fastest now.) Keeping the weight close to your body, continue to lift by pulling upwards until your upper arm is close to your ear and the weight is at chest height. Then ...

CATCH

At this point stop pulling and, very quickly, dip (by bending your knees, jumping your feet a few centimetres further apart and pushing yourself down by pushing upwards on the dumbbell), flip the wrist to knuckles-back position and 'catch' the weight at arm's length overhead. Hold this receiving position for two seconds.

RECOVERY

Straighten up, bring your feet together, hold the final position for two seconds, then lower the weight to your shoulders (using both hands), then your thighs, then lower to the floor, smoothly, by bending your knees and keeping your back flat.

Repeat with your other hand.

The power clean & jerk

This is an important power exercise for development of leg and hip muscles, lower back, trunk stabilisers, deltoids and shoulders generally – and will also develop co-ordination, timing and the catch, when done properly it gives a strong plyometric stimulus to the whole body.

*Remember that good technique is not only essential for biomechanical efficiency but for your **safety** as well!*

GET SET

Toe caps under bar, bar 3 cm from shins, shoulders higher than hips, head up, back flat, feet at hip width apart and flat on ground, over grip, knuckles outwards, hands shoulder width apart, arms straight (your arms are just taut connecting cables at this stage), shoulders in front of hands and over the bar

FIRST PULL

Ease the bar off the floor by driving through your heels: keep your head up and back flat. **Do not jerk the bar or bend your back**, arms are still cables, keep bar close to shins

SECOND PULL

The moment the bar passes knees, keeping trunk straight – with a strong pelvic thrust – push hips forwards and up so that thighs, just above the knee, actually touch the bar. The bar should be accelerating all the time; arms are still cables, head still up, no pause, rise onto toes, accelerate bar even more by 'shrugging' your shoulders and pulling upwards with arms, elbows out to the side, keep path of bar vertical and close to fully extending the body. The bar will be accelerated to just above nipple height when, at its highest point, it becomes, in fact, weightless for this split second. At that moment, and moving **very** quickly, you perform:

THE CATCH

When bar reaches nipple height, quickly bend knees, move feet a few cm farther apart and drop under bar, catching it on deltoids with elbows as high as possible, hold for a second and then:

RECOVER

Straighten legs, stand up, bring feet back to starting position, keeping elbows high and push up with your chest. Now make ready to perform the jerk

PHASE ONE

Dip: keep bar on your deltoids and keep your elbows very high (see photo), keep the feet flat, bend your knees slightly and with no delay go into:

PHASE TWO

Drive vertically with all your speed and strength so that you force bar to just above head height

PHASE THREE

As bar passes the eyes, push yourself under bar by splitting legs as per photo – do not jump up – (squatting under bar by bending both knees is acceptable for forwards but the split more closely resembles the running action and is therefore more relevant to most players) and receive bar at arms length overhead with elbows locked out and bracing yourself by reaching up high and hard. Hold for a second or two.

NB. Study the photo: in split the feet are at least 1½ times shoulder width, rear heel in line with calf, front foot turned inwards slightly for stability.

PHASE FOUR

Recovery: half step back with *front* foot first **this is a vital safety precaution**, recover back foot, hold bar for a second or two at full arms length with feet together then return safely to floor. Don't drop but go down smoothly with bar (a bar can make some noise as it lands!)

Repeat the lift, alternating feet in split so that equal training is given to both sides.

The 'Martini gym'

It's honesty time again ...

You've all heard most of the classic excuses ('I already know what I should be doing but I haven't got the time or money to invest in joining a gym' and such like). If there are any genuine problems, then there are usually ways around them. Of course they will only be effective if you genuinely want to train and aren't covering up the fact that you just can't be bothered.

In order to maintain muscle strength and mass you have to work out at least once a week, twice if you want to make gains, and a maximum of three times a week. This obviously presents a problem for those who have limited time at their disposal. Never fear – all is not lost.

myth buster

'You can train your abdominals every day ...'

Reality: It is widely believed that abdominal exercises can and should be performed on a daily basis to achieve maximum effect. You wouldn't perform squats on consecutive days, would you? So, why would you train your abdominal muscles in this way? The fact is that the abdominals can be over-trained just like any other muscle group. Muscle tissue is broken down during training, and therefore needs adequate rest and recuperation in order to regenerate. When your abdominals are trained too frequently, the recovery process is short-changed and this results in diminished muscular development. Moreover, your abdominals are also worked indirectly while training other muscle groups – they are stabilisers for virtually every movement you perform. Therefore, in effect, you get an abdominal workout every time you train. Treat your abs as you would any other muscle in your body.

TABLE 3.1 The 'Martini gym' home workout

Exercise	Kit	Method	Tips	To make it harder
Bench press	3 x *sturdy* dining chairs bin liner sports bag or backpack bricks, stones or sand for weight	Feet on one chair and hands on the other two, a little wider than shoulder width apart. Keep your body in a straight line – head, back, legs – and lower until your thumbs are parallel with your armpits, then push up	Be strict. Move down slowly and as deep as you can; hold for a split second, then up hard and fast. Concentrate on your form: keep your body in line and don't be tempted to rush or 'bounce' off the bottom of the exercise. If you want an incline press, simply elevate your feet.	A bin liner filled with stones or sand, placed in a rucksack and worn or resting between your shoulder blades will add more weight. (You won't need much – if you weigh 13.5 stones then you are already pressing around 70 kg using just your body weight.)
Pull-ups	1 x *sturdy* table or adjustable chin-up bar (available from most Argos-type catalogues or sports shops)	Lie on your back with your feet under the table. Reach up with your hands as wide as possible, hold on to the edge of the table (or the chin-up bar) and pull up until your chest meets the underside of the table. (Ideally, you should start with your hands one and a half times shoulder width apart, palms facing towards your feet.) You should pull so that your nipples stay on the same plane as your hands. Follow the same form as you would with a strict press-up: keep everything in line – head, chest, legs, etc.	You can vary the weight by bending your knees and moving your feet back towards your backside. The further away from your hands your feet are, the harder it is. Be strict: just because you are bending your legs there is no excuse to let your body sag.	Elevate your feet on a stool or a chair. (Obviously you can't go higher than the underside of the table, but that will be plenty and if it isn't then add some weight to your lap – but *keep your form*! Never sacrifice form for weight.)

Real bicep curls (i.e. not bodybuilding curls; these more closely replicate real-life demands)	1 x builder's bucket, or old suitcase bricks, stones or sand for weight 1 x wall 1 x length of rope (about 1 m)	Standing about two feet away from a wall, lean forwards and brace against it. Pick up the bucket in one hand. Starting from maximum extension, curl the bucket, at the same time drawing the elbow back and up, so that the hand moves vertically. (Note that the elbow moves back to make this curl, unlike 'normal' curls, where the forearm moves up towards the chest.) Hold at the top, and then lower slowly.	Having a problem getting full range because the edge of the bucket gets in the way? Put a rope through the handle and use that to lift the bucket. Make sure that the rope is short enough to allow full extension of the muscle without the bucket touching the floor.	Add more stones, sand, or whatever. Try to ensure that you can measure what's in the bucket. Half bricks are good for this, or if you are using sand use half an old plastic fizzy drink bottle as a measuring scoop. If you want to be posh, stick the bucket on your bathroom scales and measure it that way.
Cheat one-hand row	1 x builder's bucket, or suitcase bricks, stones or sand for weight 2 x *sturdy* chairs 1 x length of rope	Place the chairs side by side (to form a makeshift bench) and rest your left knee and left hand on them. Reach down with your right hand to pick up the bucket and pull until your hand is level with your armpit. Continue the movement through by rotating your back to lift that few extra inches, then reverse the movement slowly.	You must ensure that you really have to reach down at the start of the exercise. This may mean that you have to elevate your stance – maybe you could use a workmate instead of the chairs? You may have to use the rope to get the full range. You will have to short it, of course, but just double it round to save cutting it.	Put more in the bucket dear Liza, dear Liza . . .

TABLE 3.1 The 'Martini gym' home workout – continued

Exercise	Kit	Method	Tips	To make it harder
Upright row	1 x builder's bucket, or suitcase bricks, stones or sand for weight 1 x length of rope (about 1 m)	Stand up, with a straight back, looking straight ahead, with the bucket held in both hands, arms fully extended downwards. Pull up in one smooth action, keeping your elbows high, until your knuckles touch (or almost touch) your chin; hold, then release slowly to full extension.	Keep your elbows high and hold for a moment at the top of the exercise to squeeze those shoulders. Concentrate on form; it is all too easy to get lazy and shorten the range of movement or start leaning forwards and jerking the weight up. If this happens, lose some of the weight.	Put more weight in the bucket.
Overhead press	1 x wall	Kneel down, ankles together, with the soles of your feet pressed against the bottom of the wall. Put your hands on the floor, thumbs together, about a foot in front of your knees. Put your head on the floor between your index fingers. Keeping your hands, feet and head where they are, straighten your legs. Your body weight is now directly over your hands – straighten your arms to perform an overhead press.	Be strict: down slowly, hold for a split second, then up hard and fast. If you are struggling with the weight, move your hands forwards, away from your knees, and the weight will reduce. You can also widen the space between your hands to reduce the weight.	The closer your hands are to your knees, the heavier the weight. To keep a record of your progress, measure how far your hands are from your knees; you can progress in stages by moving your hands one inch closer to your knees.

Dips	3 x *sturdy* dining chairs, bin liner, sports bag or backpack bricks, stones or sand for weight	Set up the chairs as for the bench press: feet up on one chair, hands just to the sides and rear of your hips on the other two. Dip as low as possible – *slowly*; hold, then drive up to full extension, hard and fast. Hold again, then repeat.	Concentrate on form and getting full extension on every rep.	Use a backpack or bag filled with a bin liner of stones or sand to add weight (as for the bench press), but this time rest the weight in your lap. Remember to measure the weight used and record your progress. Alternatively, the corner where two parts of the kitchen work surface meet at a right angle makes a great dip rack.
Sides and fronts	2 x bricks	Raise the weights (bricks) out in front of you until your arms are straight and parallel with the floor. At the top of the exercise, ensure that your thumbs are pointing dead ahead. Return to the start, then raise the weights out to your sides, in line with your body, so that your arms are, again, straight and parallel to the floor. At the top of this part of the exercise, ensure that your thumbs are pointing straight down.	Concentrate on form (i.e. where your thumbs are pointing).	Try different types of brick. 'Common' bricks are not as heavy as 'paviours' and 'engineer blues' are heavier still.

You can establish a perfectly good gym at home: the 'Martini gym' (so-called because, like the drink of that name, it can be used 'any time, any place anywhere'). It will cost you nothing and, as you can use it without leaving home, it has a double benefit. You can have a workout and be in the shower inside an hour. You can even do it while baby-sitting: exercise and brownie points!

Even if you can only grab half an hour three times a week, that's enough to maintain upper body muscle fitness. If you can schedule yourself two one-hour sessions then you're laughing.

Here's how. Table 3.1 lists the key exercises and give details of how you can improvise. If the kit specified doesn't quite work for you, then adapt it or change it, but don't use it as an excuse to do nothing. *Remember, be honest ...*

Shopping list

You will need a bit of kit to do the following 'Martini gym' workouts, but it can all be scavenged or found at car boot sales.

- 25 kg of sand
- 12 x 'common' house bricks
- 1 x old backpack or sports bag
- 1 x old small suitcase or hard briefcase
- 1 x bin liner
- 1 m rope (enough to take your body weight)
- 1 x bathroom scales

Everything else listed in Table 3.1 can be found in or around the house.

top tip If you are struggling with the bucket try to get hold of an old briefcase or suitcase and use that instead. Because it is slimmer, this means that your hand will stay closer to your body during the lifts, which you may find easier. If you are not a fan of physical comedy, an old belt or rope will ensure that it doesn't fall open unexpectedly.

Legs

Legs are always going to be a problem if you can't get to a gym. However, it's not impossible to train them well if you have commitment and imagination. Be creative, try things – it's good for the soul.

Squats and calf raises

If you've got a training partner then piggybacks will suffice. Keep an eye on your form and communicate at all times. Be careful about going too deep with someone on your back; even with the best partner the load is very unsteady and will place a major strain on your knees.

World's strongest man

How about the family car? Find someone to mind the hand brake and steer, and with a rolled-up towel as a pad and your shoulder against the bumper, off you go! You can adjust the resistance by engaging the hand brake slightly while you are pushing. With a bit of practice you can find the best way to get a good-quality leg workout (e.g. 6 x 10 m reps). In fact, this probably offers a closer match to the action required on the pitch than anything you could do in the gym.

Skipping

A perfectly good skipping rope can be made from a length of washing line. If you want to get sexy, then a couple of bits of broom handle with washers screwed into the ends will hold the 'rope' and help it turn freely.

Olympic lifts

A trip to your local car boot sale is likely to provide you with a barbell, dumbbells and weights. They will almost certainly be one-inch diameter with smaller weights. You can create your own Olympic bar by making two discs of nine-inch diameter to fit on either end (as described earlier). As your technique improves, just add weights to the bar and you can practise the one-hand snatch and the power clean and jerk to your heart's content.

Speed and running fitness (cardiovascular conditioning)

This section looks at three elements:

1. **basic stamina** – the ability to perform for long periods at low/moderate intensity
2. **speed** – the ability to go fast for short periods
3. **speed endurance** – the ability to operate at medium/high levels repeatedly.

Basic stamina

Stamina is the ability to keep going at a moderate rate for long periods. It will improve the body's ability to flush out waste products (oxidants) effectively; these are produced during short-burst intensive periods (e.g. sprints).

When performed at the correct rate and for a long enough period of time, fat reserves will be burnt (when you are using more calories than have been taken on).

It will be important to measure and record heart rate here to ensure that you are operating at the correct intensity. Too fast and you are defeating the object because you will be burning sugars and producing oxidants. Too slow and you will not be working your heart hard enough.

What we are looking for is a slow jog (preferably on grass to lessen the impact on the joints) building from 16 minutes to 40 minutes over a period of weeks. (To keep variety you can swim or cycle – anything is OK as long as it is done at a consistent intensity (so five-a-side football would not be suitable).

Note that when you get the pace right you are likely to find it unnaturally slow. Don't worry: it is. Keep boredom to a minimum by splitting the run into two: eight minutes out, eight minutes back.

There is no real need to warm up as the run is at such a low impact. It is a good exercise to fit into your 'dead time' as, including a shower, you can do it in a lunch hour. If you are really pushed for time, you can also split 30 minutes' aerobic training into 2 x 15-minute bouts during the day and you will get virtually the same benefit.

Measuring your heart rate

The heart rate you should maintain during the basic stamina phase is called your 'target heart rate'. There are several ways of arriving at this figure. Some methods for calculating the target rate take individual differences into consideration; here is one of them.

1. Subtract your age from 220 to find your maximum heart rate.
2. Subtract your *resting heart rate* from your *maximum heart rate* to determine your *heart rate reserve*. (Your resting heart rate can be determined by taking your pulse after sitting quietly for five minutes, before you undertake any exercise. The best time is when you are still in bed in the morning; although, if woken by an alarm, you should wait about five minutes.)
3. Take 70 per cent of your *heart rate reserve* to determine your *heart rate raise*.
4. Add your *heart rate raise* to your *resting heart rate* to find your *target heart rate*.

TABLE 3.2 Example of a target heart rate calculation

Maximum heart rate	220
Minus age	24
= total	196
Minus resting heart rate	60
= heart rate reserve	136
Divide by 70% or multiply by 0.7	
= heart rate raise	95
Heart rate raise + resting heart rate	
= target rate	155

Count your pulse for 10 seconds and multiply by six to get the per-minute rate.

When checking your heart rate during a workout, take your pulse within five seconds after interrupting exercise because it starts to go down as soon you stop moving.

Speed work

An overview of the mechanics of speed and agility

Forward movement is achieved by the extension of the hip, knee and ankle joints: the 'drive' phase (action 1 in the accompanying illustration).

Sprinting is doing the same thing very fast, repeating it with alternate legs more than four times each second. Apart from a slight cross-body arm action, there should be no side-to-side movement.

As the driving foot leaves the ground, the heel of that foot should fold fast and touch the buttock, the leg coming through as a short (and therefore fast) lever (action 2).

The folded leg should be pulled through, as in action 3 to action 4, to a high knee lift that will impart a 'ground reaction' and make the power of the other leg, which is now driving, more effective.

As the foot returns to the ground, it should be pulled back to make a dynamic 'active' landing.

Powerful drive and subsequent relaxation of the driving muscles will make the foot fold to the buttock; it will make the knee come through fast and high and the pendulum effect will aid in making the active landing.

The arms should work as opposites to the legs; they should balance and guide the whole action – no flapping, no excessive opening and closing of the elbows (which should be kept at roughly 90 degrees) and the elbows driven back – all the best work in sprinting is done behind the body.

Forward speed is the product of stride rate and stride range. A stride range or length of two metres and a stride rate of two metres per second will give a forward velocity of eight metres per second, which equals 100 metres in 12.5 seconds – a time of which any self-respecting prop would be proud.

Speed of muscular contraction is largely (genetically) determined by the percentage of white (fast) and red (slower) fibres found in the muscle itself. There are many other factors that influence speed: muscle fuels available, co-ordination, flexibility and muscle viscosity, gross, relative and specific strength, elastic and starting strength, correct motor programmes in the brain, motivation, an absence of wasted movement ... and many more.

This means that diet must be good; training must start with the general and become more specific (never forgetting speed – if you forget speed, you can forget winning!); good stretching and warm-up procedures *must* be followed; multi-exercise circuits *and* correct (free) weight training must be undertaken; drills must be perfect; short sprints must be undertaken regularly; sloppy practice must be ruthlessly stamped out, and good style inculcated.

However, note that acceleration, the ability to change pace, and physical and mental toughness are often more important than a high top speed.

Sprinting drills

Well, that's the science bit, but how do you improve your pace?

The 'drills' described on the following pages are designed to improve both your rate and range of stride; the movements are fast and light at the start, stronger and more powerful at the end.

Introduce the drills gradually (remember golden rule 2 – pace yourself). We have seen big strong men reduced to tears by the too rapid introduction of these drills: 'shin splints' can cripple a player, ruin their season and any chance of advancement (big, heavy athletes tend to suffer more than lighter ones). Once you have suffered from such injuries, they tend to recur, so be careful and take things gradually.

There is no need to measure your heart rate here; what we are talking about is flat-out speed. These will be short, high-quality sessions that can precede a short weights session. Don't do them the day after a heavy legs workout. The emphasis is on quality and teaching your legs to go faster, so make sure you are well rested.

If you have ignored the call for quality until now, please register it immediately! These drills are the place where you teach your body to propel you fast. Just as a top-class musician will never rush through their scales, a top-class athlete has no time for sub-standard drills.

Warm-up

The same principles apply as those employed at the gym. A fair warm-up need not take more than 20–25 minutes but will save you a world of pain in terms of injury.

An example of a warm-up routine is:

- 10 minutes' running (two laps of a pitch/track at a jog, then stride out the lengths/straights on one more lap)
- stretching and drills – in pairs
- remember to prepare the muscle that is to be extended by stretching before you carry out the drill.

Drills

These drills will be used and referred to in the phased workouts in the next chapter of this book.

Heel pick-up

How to do it

Body upright, waist long, thigh vertical, *fast* pick-up of heels to backside (so that contact can be heard); use different rhythms throughout to avoid motor stereotypes but keep the number of lifts per leg equal (e.g. L, L, R, L, R, R, R, L, R, L, R, L, etc.)

Purpose

Conditioning of hamstrings, learning to make recovery leg a short (and therefore fast) lever

Knee pick-up

How to do it

Good posture, knees pulled fast and high to chest, keep thighs in line of running (don't splay the knees)

Purpose

Conditioning hip flexors, learning to lift knees fast and high in running action to aid stride length and improve ground reaction

Side steps

How to do it

Good posture, side skipping, aim for height/distance on each step, keep body square to line of travel (looking back helps), stay on balls of feet

Purpose

General agility, conditioning of the groin (adductors and abductors) to avoid imbalance and injury, and provide stabilisation of prime movers

High skipping

How to do it
Good tall posture, top of head high, aim for greatest possible height and knee lift with front leg raised so that soles of shoes are visible to observers in front

Purpose
Conditioning of hip flexors and extensors, and calf muscles to teach forceful and short ground contact time

Leg raises

How to do it:
Legs straight (or high kicking, chorus-girl style)

Purpose
To condition hip flexors and give dynamic stretch to hamstrings

Note: the leg comes towards the chest, not the other way around. Keep your chest upright throughout the drill.

Bounding

How to do it

The most important drill of all! Body upright, take a series of long-jump 'take-offs' with one short running step between each; aim for height and 'air time' on each take-off

Purpose

Conditioning of hip extensors, hip flexors, trunk stabilisers, calf muscles, to teach forceful drive and knee lift

Speed sessions

What you are looking for here is to train your body to go *fast*. So you need to do these exercises when you are reasonably fresh, and you must allow yourself plenty of rest between sets to ensure that every set is *top* quality. If you do these drills when you are tired, you will never get the feeling of travelling fast.

During each of the drills you need to concentrate on developing a marked change of pace. Concentrate on how it feels. When you accelerate, drop your hands and lean forwards slightly; this will help to ensure that the power your legs are delivering is propelling you forwards.

Hollow sprints

Roughly mark out 40 m into 10 m sets (i.e. you will have the start and then four further markers). Accelerate gently over the first 10 m to full pace when you get to the first marker, flat out to the second marker, decelerate to three-quarters pace after marker three and hold until the last maker where you accelerate to full pace until the finish line. (This drill is just as easy to do between fence posts or lamp posts as it is between markers on a track.)

10 m	20 m	30 m	40 m
Accelerate >>>>>>>	Sprint >>>>>>>>>>	Coast >>>>>>>>>>	Sprint >>>>>>>>

Back to backs

Nothing too complicated here. Roughly mark out a 35 m distance with markers at 10 m, 25 m and the end (35 m). Gently accelerate up to the start of the 10 m then eye-balls out for the next 15 m (to the 25 m marker); use the next 10 m (to the 35 m marker) to decelerate, turn straight round and start accelerating to the 'start line' again, etc. There and back is one rep. Check your middle 15 m times and go hard for three reps. Increase the reps by one or two per session, keeping your middle 15 m time as constant as possible.

10 m 25 m 35 m
Accelerate >>>>>>> Sprint >>>>>>>>>> Decelerate >>>>>
<<<<<< Decelerate <<<<<<<<<<<<< Sprint<<<<< Accelerate

Slaloms

These are just as the name suggests. Set up a slalom route with a 20 m straight on the way out and 20 m worth of 'weaving' on the way back. Go eyeballs out all the way and check your time. Jog to recover (i.e. until your heart rate is back to around 120 bpm) and repeat.

Start with two reps, record your average time and try to increase by one rep per week up to a maximum of six. Try to beat your time.

Pursuits

You'll need a partner for this. Set a 25m course (either straight or slalom). You go from a standing start and your partner starts ten metres behind you. You go when he passes you. The aim is to give you a target to chase. (You can make it interesting by having a little side bet if you so wish...)

Speed stamina

The following exercises stress the heart, lungs and body over a longer period to more intense levels. Some routines you can use are described below.

300 m reps

Start with one rep at a comfortable pace in week one. Beat the time in week two. Add another rep in week three at the same pace, and so on. Work up to three reps in a session.

150 m reps

You are looking to build up to five reps at a heart rate of around 90 per cent of maximum, with as long a recovery as is required to get your breathing back to normal. (Take an average of your five rep times and use that as your target to beat every session.)

Fartlek

Go for 50 m at about three-quarters pace, 50 m at a jog, 50 m at three-quarters pace, 50 m at a jog, and so on, back to back. If you are using a track it's fairly straightforward. If not, use a rugby pitch – three-quarter pace the diagonals between the 22 m and 15 m lines then jog an imaginary curve behind the posts, then off again. If you can't get to a pitch then why not try using lamp posts as markers?

Recovery

Do 50 m reps at a heart rate of around 90 per cent of maximum, record your time and then the time it takes for your heart rate to come back down to around 120 bpm. Then off again. Start at 10 reps, then work up by two more per week to a maximum of 20.

Speed and cardio training away from the gym: saved by skipping

It's going to be a bit of a trial to do your stamina run if you are baby-sitting, and 300 times round the lounge or sprinting up and down a hotel corridor is not really advisable.

No problem. Even if you are staying away from home you can carry an excellent workout in your briefcase – the skipping rope. Skipping has long been used by athletes who seek to develop hand/eye co-ordination as well as speed and stamina. Boxers, sprinters, weightlifters, tennis players and professional rugby players from both codes all use skipping extensively.

Here are some basics you can incorporate into your weekly workouts. They are also a great fallback when time or space is at a premium.

Type of rope

There are many different ropes out there but for our purposes use either a leather rope (prepare it as described earlier) or a speed rope made from plastic. If you choose a speed rope, try to get one with ball bearings in the handle so that it is less likely to foul.

Measuring the rope

For our purposes the ideal length can be judged in the following way: hold the rope handles in your right hand and put your left foot in the rope to keep it on the floor. Pull the rope taut and if the tops of the handles come to the top of your left shoulder then it is spot on.

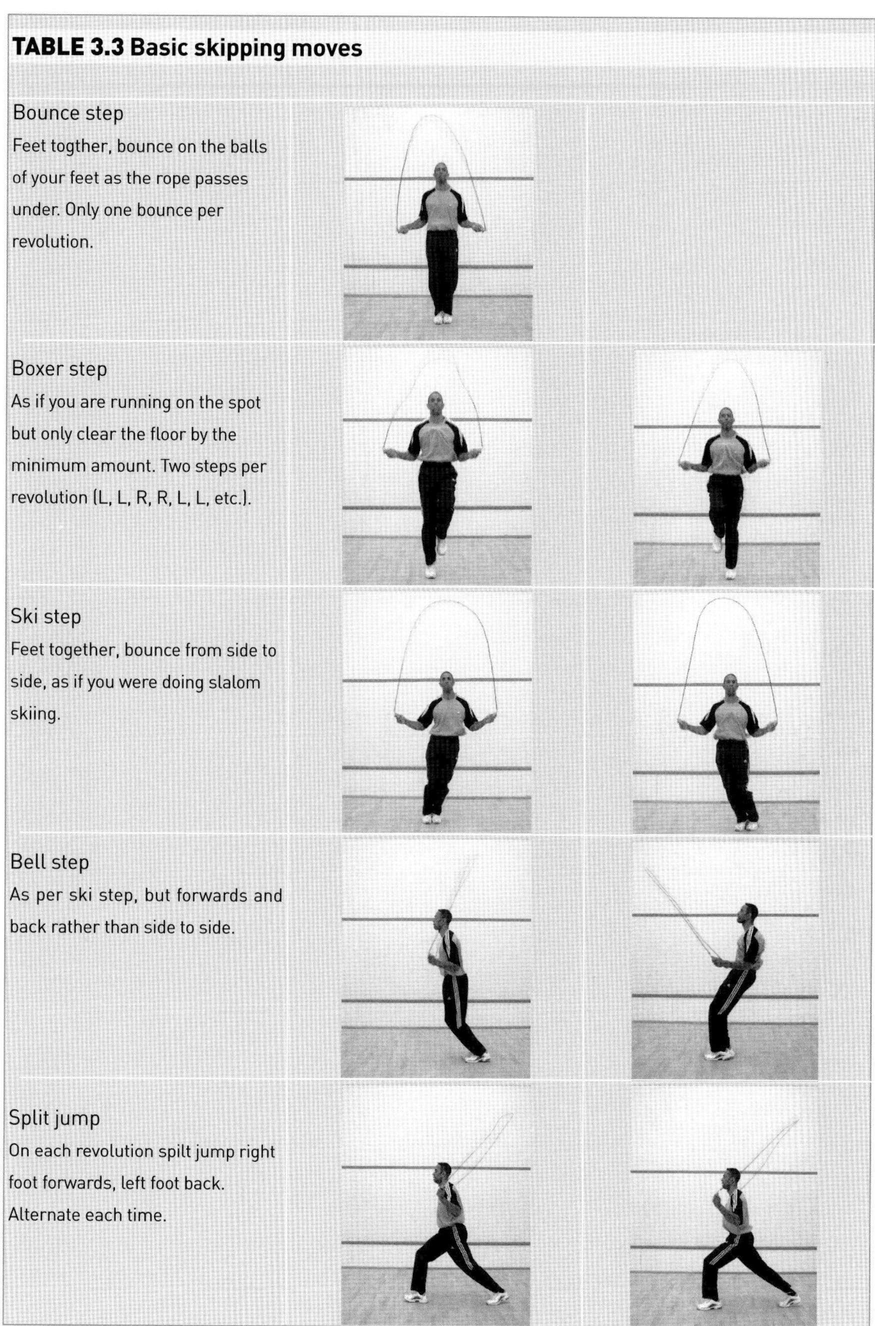

TABLE 3.3 Basic skipping moves

Move	Description
Bounce step	Feet togther, bounce on the balls of your feet as the rope passes under. Only one bounce per revolution.
Boxer step	As if you are running on the spot but only clear the floor by the minimum amount. Two steps per revolution (L, L, R, R, L, L, etc.).
Ski step	Feet together, bounce from side to side, as if you were doing slalom skiing.
Bell step	As per ski step, but forwards and back rather than side to side.
Split jump	On each revolution spilt jump right foot forwards, left foot back. Alternate each time.

If, after this you want some tricks (crossovers, side swings, etc.) then ask any self-respecting school child or boxer. They will be glad to help.

Progression

Your basis should be as follows. Your skipping speed should be about 100 turns per minute, and no faster than 100 turns in 45 seconds. If you can comfortably complete stage 1, move on to stage 2, and so on. Remember, *progression is everything*.

Here are the stages:

1. 5 x 100 bounce steps
2. 2 x 250 bounce steps
3. 1 x 500 bounce steps
4. 5 minutes alternating each of the steps in Table 3.3 in sets of four (e.g. bounce x 4, boxer x 4, bounce x 4, bell x 4, bounce x 4, ski x 4 etc.)
5. gradually increase by 30 seconds each time; this will provide you with an excellent cardiovascular workout.

Routines

Sprint routines

After a steady warm-up of five minutes, change the step to a running action (like boxer step only with one jump per revolution). Turn the rope as fast as possible and pick up your knees in a sprinting movement for 10 seconds (count the revolutions in that time). Then slow the rope to warm-up pace and continue for 100 turns. Repeat three times and then rest.

This routine can be progressed by reducing the recovery from 100 to 90, 80, and so on, and by increasing the sprints by one repetition each time to a maximum of six. Try and increase your speed (i.e. the number of revolutions in the 10-second sprint).

Speed endurance routines

As above, but sprint at three-quarters pace for 20 seconds and recover with 100 turns. Repeat five times.

Progress by reducing the recovery by five turns each time and increasing the number of repetitions to a maximum of 10.

Plyometrics

> Important warning: *high-impact plyometric work can be unsafe for people with back and/or joint wear, and can place major stress on tendons in the over-21 age group or the still-growing group. Short time/lower load exercises would be more appropriate.*

This is a massive topic and one on which whole books are written. We have included a concise overview of the relevant bits that will get you started and add benefit and variety to your workouts.

Plyometrics is a form of conditioning that seeks to improve the muscle's ability to recruit and deploy maximum muscle action in the shortest time possible. It is therefore excellent for training speed and power within rugby.

Although plyometric exercises take different forms, the objectives can be split into two groups for our purposes:

1. **starting strength** – the ability to instantaneously recruit the maximum number of muscle fibres possible (e.g. an initial burst of speed from standing or slow pace to flat out)
2. **explosive stamina** – the ability to maintain the initial explosion of muscle contraction going over a period or distance against some resistance (e.g. tackling, busting tackles, driving in a ruck or maul, etc.).

What follows are some basic groups of drills that will attack the upper and lower body requirements of our sport. All of the following should be done on a forgiving surface (e.g. grass or a running track), *never on tarmac*.

Knee tucks

TECHNIQUE

- Drop to a half squat and immediately explode upwards into a tuck jump.
- Land as per jump squats (see earlier).
- On touching the ground, treat it as if it were red hot and drive upwards into another tuck jump.
- Initially perform two sets of 10 tucks with two minutes' rest between sets.
- When you've got the technique nailed, build up to four sets of 20 with one minute between sets.
- Progress gradually to six sets with a one-minute rest between sets.

Multiple bounds

TECHNIQUE

- Jog in slowly, the trunk vertical, and then make flat-footed bounds.
- Maintain good posture throughout, stressing high knee action and powerful drives from the grounded leg.
- Perform three sets over 20 m with two minutes' rest.
- Build gradually to six sets over 50 m with one minute's rest.

Split jumps

TECHNIQUE

- Starting position: large stride to the front, one leg fully extended and the other at 90 degrees.
- Spring up powerfully and, changing legs, land back at the starting position. Do once on each leg for one rep.
- Perform two sets of five jumps (each side) with two minutes' rest between sets.
- Build gradually to four sets of 10 jumps (each side) with one minute's rest between sets.

Power skipping

TECHNIQUE

- With your skipping rope, start with four standard bounce steps.
- On the fifth step explode upwards and turn the rope fast so that it passes twice under your feet before you land.
- Do four more bounce steps and repeat.
- Perform three repetitions and then recover skip for 100 turns; this is one set.
- Do three sets and then rest.
- Progress by reducing the recovery by 10 turns and reducing the standard bounce steps to three between power jumps.
- When you can comfortably complete three power jumps with no break and only 50 turns' recovery, increase by one power jump per set.

Speed loading (resistance)

It is not uncommon for coaches and players to believe that if you run up enough steep hills then, as your legs become stronger, you will consequently move faster. Not true. If it were, then we would see fell runners winning the 100 m gold medal at the Olympics.

Resistance work is an important part of a conditioning programme, but it should be viewed as only one of many aspects. You will get most out of this section of your work if you remember to:

use light resistance to ensure that sprinting form is not affected.

This means that near-vertical hills or 50 kg rucksacks are counter-productive. All they teach your legs to do is to run up near-vertical hills or carry 50 kg rucksacks. You need to learn to go fast! Here are a couple of ideas that will provide moderate overload while allowing you to maintain good form. There are plenty of others involving varying degrees and types of equipment. Understand the principle and then, if you like, try some ideas of your own.

DIY resistance equipment (version 1)

An ordinary car tyre (no wheel!) gives enough resistance for our purpose (and not a Mini tyre either – an old Land Rover front tyre would be best – large enough to provide good resistance and not bounce all over the place). Tie one end to a five-metre length of rope and attach the other to a weight belt or piece of seat belt (or

something similar) tied around your waist. (When sprinting with this kit, make sure that the rope is taut before you set off, to avoid jarring.)

If you have a training partner then you can use the harness and rope to apply variable resistance.

When using the harness in this way you should gradually increase resistance over 15–20 metres. Start with only just keeping the rope taut and steadily increase the pressure until the runner is hardly moving forward at the finish point.

DIY resistance equipment (version 2)

If you want something a bit more portable, try making a drag-parachute. Again, take a five-metre length of lightweight but strong cord (if the cord is too heavy this will not work; if the string can take 10 kg it will be fine) and attach one end to a piece of seat belt (or similar) tied around your waist. Then take an old single bed sheet and cut it to make a square approximately 1.5 m square. Fold it twice diagonally (to make a triangle) and cut off the top centimetre; this will make a hole in the middle, which will help to stabilise the chute in use and stop it tumbling.

Take another two pieces of cord – each three metres in length – and tie them to opposite corners of your square of fabric, creating two loops. Tie the free end of your five-metre cord to the point where these two three-metre lengths cross. (You need to be reasonably accurate in joining these at the centre to ensure that the chute is balanced.) To use the chute, stretch it out behind you and get sprinting!

Health warning: a sudden gust of wind can destabilise your running action and therefore put stresses on knees, etc. If you have any concerns about your ability to withstand such effects, then avoid this exercise – *and any contact sport* – until it is fixed.

DIY resistance equipment (version 3)

The simplest of all! Incline (not hills) running will offer a similar degree of overload. With each of these drills, start with two reps of 30 m and build up to a maximum of six reps of 60 m.

This may not seem very far, but if you consider how far you would run in a game of rugby you will realise that sprinting for more than about 30 m will happen just once or twice per season and, if you go any further than that, you will probably find yourself standing in the club car park.

4 WALLS, ROOF AND WINDOWS putting it all together

aim:

- To provide you with a three-phase structure for pre- and in-season training; you will utilise all the elements and tools described in the earlier chapters.

Before you start

The nature of your training has to change as you approach the start of the season, and it needs to change again during the competitive months. You therefore need to consider a 'phased' approach, as outlined in this chapter.

Very important note

Under no circumstances should you attempt the exercises in phase two before you have completed phase one. The three-phase approach to conditioning presented in this chapter has been developed scientifically over many years. It is designed to be progressively demanding and if you jump ahead without stabilising your technique or core strength, then the only short-cut you will make will be to the physio's bench or worse. So, once again, remember the three golden rules:

1. be honest
2. pace yourself
3. quality before quantity – *always*.

It is important that you tailor your own programme. Think about what you need for your position. Whatever conditioning routine you undertake, you should constantly refer back to how that will fit the demands of your position and the specific objectives you have set yourself for improvement. (This is obviously a base from which to build, and overall speed and power should be common to all positions.)

A good way to do this is to watch a couple of matches on video that feature a player you admire. Concentrate on them and make a rough note of things such as:

- **sprinting patterns**

  – what distances do they sprint/jog/run?

  – how many times do they repeat these distances in each half?

  – do they sprint from a standing start (e.g. scrum half) or from a roll (e.g. fullback)?

  – do they run in straight lines or curves, at angles, etc.?

- **strength patterns**

  – what tasks do they perform and how often (e.g. ripping and mauling are going to involve plenty of push/pull upper body strength)?

  – do they have to perform strength tasks at speed (hand-off) or from a set position (scrummaging)?

Phase one

This is the foundation on which we will build. You are going to ingrain the speed and strength drills – in effect, you are training to train.

Duration: six weeks (May to mid-June, assuming that this is prior to the commencement of pre-season training with your club).

Aim: improvement in technique, general strength, strength endurance, basic fitness.

Start and finish phase one by carrying out the three tests listed below (and described earlier). If you are approaching this scheme from a low basis of fitness you should leave the tests until week four, by which time your body will be back into the swing of things. The three tests, as you will no doubt remember, are:

- test Quadrathlon
- 120 m time trial
- Harvard step test.

Repeat these tests once every three weeks throughout phase one.

TABLE 4.1 Example of a phase one record sheet (tests)

Date (week commencing)	Body weight	Standing long jump	Three jumps	30m sprint	Overhead shot throw	Quad score	Speed and speed endurance			Harvard step test
10/10/2004	85 kg	2.09 m	6.23 m	4.7 sec	10.86 m	41	5.1 40 m	5.4 80 m	6.5 120 m	38 pts
1							40 m	80 m	120 m	
2							40 m	80 m	120 m	

Strength

The objective of the phase one strength routines is to build all-over strength and co-ordination while stabilising technique.

Even if you are a very experienced weight trainer, do not skip this, or any other, stage. These three phases are designed to complement each other and if you ignore any one stage it will come back and bite you later. The scheme is a single-set routine, but based on compound, multi-joint exercises, and will encourage your muscles to work as a team rather than on their own.

The first few sessions will be somewhat experimental; the number of repetitions will be different depending on your objectives. Unless you are looking to put weight on, then do no more than 10 repetitions of any one exercise.

Work through in the order given, but for variety you can start each session at a different point in the routine. *Do one set of each exercise only.*

Notice that the multi-joint (compound), large-muscle-mass exercises are used first, the single-joint exercises next, and the abdominal and trunk exercises last.

When using dumbbells, always start the set with the weaker arm and only complete the same amount of repetitions on your stronger arm. In this way both sides can be balanced.

Never bench press without a spotter. If you slip and you're lucky, you'll smash your mouth, teeth and jaw. If you're unlucky, you'll crush your larynx and die.

Women have a more vulnerable back than men. (This is just the way that the different bodies are designed.) If you are a woman, it's even more important that you strengthen the whole girdle of muscles around your middle, so study the core stability exercises detailed in Chapter 2. Start off with two or three reps, and build up by one repetition each session until you reach 20 reps.

Phase one lasts for six weeks, and should be done three times a week. Start sensibly. This means that you don't work so hard that you're too stiff to train the next day; that would be stupid. By the end of the six weeks you should have raised the weight on every exercise several times and be working so hard that you really need to scream and shout to get the last reps out. No dainty effort and pretty Lycra posing for us!

And yes, there are many more exercises than those here. That's not the point, though. This is a time-management, common-sense schedule and the exercises chosen have been carefully and scientifically selected to give the best possible results in the least time. Remember, you are a rugby player, not a gym rat, body-builder or weight lifter.

Note well: six weeks is not enough to stabilise your technique on the Olympic lifts, so only lift what you can actually manage with good technique – no maximum attempts yet.

Abs

As this is such an important area we have given it its own section in each of the three phases. Each phase, *if completed strictly and at a consistently high quality*, will prepare you for the rigours to come. One thing to note: if these exercises feel easy, then you are not doing them correctly. Remember golden rule three? Quality before quantity – *always*.

Ab curls (these are not sit-ups)

Start position

Lie flat on your back, with a *neutral spine*, heels on the floor; place your hands on your thighs – arms straight

How to do it

Breathe out and pull your navel towards your spine (this will brace your muscles); now, *concentrate* on using only the muscles in your stomach to *curl* your shoulders off the floor; slide your hands up your thighs until your shoulders are clear of the floor; hold for a good second and then return slowly to the start; this is one repetition

The movement that you are looking for is a curl, not a sit-up. This a very subtle, slow and steady movement (at an even tempo, up and down), and controlled throughout.

Lying sides

Start position

Lie flat on your side, top arm resting along your side (the other arm can be beneath you in any way that is comfortable); your back, chest and legs should all be in a straight line throughout

How to do it

Breathe out and pull your navel towards your spine (this will brace your muscles); now, *concentrate* on using only the muscles in your side to lift your legs clear of the floor; hold for a second and then return slowly to the start; this is one repetition

Concentrate on keeping your body straight. Imagine that you are being squeezed between two boards and so you body and legs cannot move forwards or back, only up and down. If, after about eight to ten repetitions you cannot feel your obliques (sides) working then you are probably not performing this exercise correctly.

Plank

Start position

Perform a bridge press-up resting your weight on your elbows rather than your hands; concentrate on ensuring that your back and legs are in a straight line (see above)

How to do it

Start the exercise by bracing your abs and back; breathe out and then *slowly* raise your right leg, keeping it straight until your thigh is parallel with the floor; hold and return *slowly* to the starting position; if your back sags or your pelvis twists during the exercise then it does not count – *only strict form counts*; when you have performed one on either side this is a single repetition

A good tip for this exercise is to imagine that you have a brimful glass of water balancing on each buttock. If, when you raise your leg, your hips sag to the floor or you have to tilt your pelvis to raise the leg, then the water will spill and you are not doing the exercise correctly. The whole object of these types of exercise is to train your abdomen (your 'core') to be able to lock and hold your weight when you are performing.

Running work

There is going to be a concentration on aerobic development here, but coupled with the drills you will have an excellent foundation on which to build fast, strong running actions.

Drills

Look back to the drills section (in Chapter 3) and start by performing the drill and stretch routines over 15 metres. Concentrate on perfect form and carry out each exercise once. You are your own personal trainer, so demonstrate perfect technique to yourself *every time*. After week three the techniques should be starting to become ingrained, so you can increase the distance over which they are performed to 20 metres.

Speed work

The emphasis here is on short, high-quality speed work. For this you can use any of the sprint routines mentioned earlier or short sessions of touch rugby. If you and some friends play touch rugby, then ensure that there are lots of short sprints involved, interspersed with plenty of rest. Try eight rounds of three minutes on a pitch with lots of space. A good example would be six-a-side across the pitch, from 22 m marker to tryline, using the 15 m marks as trylines.

Aerobic work

Work within your training zone (see the section in Chapter 3 on monitoring your heart rate to find out what this is). Start with a steady 20-minute run twice a week and build up in four-minute increments to no more than 40 minutes twice a week.

Record-keeping

Tables 4.2 and 4.3 are, respectively, examples of a record chart and a training diary; they are included to show you that progress happens in real life. You might like to take a photocopy of the record sheet (Table 4.2) so that you can fill it in as you go and note your own progress. Always start with relatively easy loads and don't increase them by too much. That way you guarantee improvement and you won't be discouraged. Remember, when you can do 10 reps, increase the load; if you can't do 10, stay on that load and increase the number of reps until you can. Keep records of your running and speed exercises in your diary (like the example in Table 4.3) and always keep your record sheets and your diary together.

TABLE 4.2 Phase one record sheet

Phase one	Date: Reps	Weight	Date: Reps	Weight	Date: Reps	Weight	Date: Reps	Weight	Date: Reps	Weight	Date: Reps	Weight
One-hand power snatch		kg		kg		kg		kg		kg		kg
Power clean and jerk		kg		kg		kg		kg		kg		kg
Bench press		kg		kg		kg		kg		kg		kg
Cheat one-hand row		kg		kg		kg		kg		kg		kg
Alternate dumbbell press		kg		kg		kg		kg		kg		kg
Pull-ups		Body weight		Body weight		Body weight		Body weight		Body weight		Body weight
Dips		kg		kg		kg		kg		kg		kg
Upright row		kg		kg		kg		kg		kg		kg
Sides and fronts		kg		kg		kg		kg		kg		kg
Screw curls		kg		kg		kg		kg		kg		kg
Tri-press		kg		kg		kg		kg		kg		kg
Ab curls		Body weight		Body weight		Body weight		Body weight		Body weight		Body weight
Lying sides		Body weight		Body weight		Body weight		Body weight		Body weight		Body weight
Plank		Body weight		Body weight		Body weight		Body weight		Body weight		Body weight

TABLE 4.3 Example of a phase one training diary

MONDAY Rest
TUESDAY 20-min easy jog Drills + touch Weight session
WEDNESDAY Rest
THURSDAY 20-min easy jog Drills + sprints Weight session
FRIDAY Rest
SATURDAY 22-min easy jog Drills + skills Weight session
SUNDAY 22-min run, ride bike or swim (very low intensity – this is active rest and very important)
NOTES

TABLE 4.3 Example of a phase one training diary – continued

MONDAY Rest
TUESDAY Evening: 22-min easy jog Drills + sprints
WEDNESDAY Lunchtime: Weight session (45-min)
THURSDAY Evening: 22-min easy jog Drills + skills Weight session
FRIDAY Rest
SATURDAY Afternoon: 24-min easy jog Drills + hour touch rugby with friends Weight session
SUNDAY 24-min run, ride bike or swim
NOTES

MONDAY

Weights, a few max one-hand snatch, bench press or other exercises: be creative.

TUESDAY

24-min run

WEDNESDAY

Evening: 22-min easy jog

Drills + skills

Weight session

THURSDAY

Lunchtime: Weight session

FRIDAY

SATURDAY

SUNDAY

NOTES

Increase the distance you run by two minutes a week (you'll soon be up to 40 minutes and that's enough).

The emphasis in phase one is on fitness, general stamina, ingrained skill and increases in strength: you are *training to train.*

Include at least two speed units in your training each week: if you ever forget speed you can forget winning.

Speed kills! Other people if you have it; you if you don't.

Phase two

This part is all about strength and speed.
Duration: six weeks (mid-June to end of July).
Aim: improvement in your absolute and elastic strength, and your ability to express power. In other words, your ability to be strong and to deliver that power *fast*.

Begin phase two with the tests below. Test yourself again regularly and take a pride in your progress. Remember: only improvement matters.

The tests

These follow a thorough warm-up routine and should be carried out when you are fresh and rested – not the day after a match or a heavy session. To reiterate, they should only be undertaken *when you have warmed up thoroughly*.

1. **Body weight** – weigh yourself, but only once a month (do not start to obsess).
2. **Long-arm pull-up** – maximum number with strict form.
3. **Max flat bench press** – single rep (and use a spotter). Build up to the max attempt and record as a percentage of your body weight.
4. **Test Quadrathlon**.
5. **Speed and speed endurance** – carry out the 120 m sprint as outlined in Chapter 2 and record each 40 m section as a separate time; keep an eye on the relative speeds between the 80 m and 120 m time, and the absolute time for the 40 m.
6. **Harvard step test** – try to be consistent; you have worked up to a distance that takes you about 40 minutes at a steady-state pace; maintain the distance and seek to reduce the time without raising your heart rate.

These tests should be repeated every two weeks throughout phases two and three. Again, you may wish to use the sample record sheet in Table 4.4 as a template that you can fill in to record your progress.

TABLE 4.4 Phase two and three record sheets (tests)

Date (week commencing)	Body weight	Long-arm pull-ups	Max. flat bench press (barbell)	Standing long jump	Three jumps	30m sprint	Overhead shot throw	Quad score	Speed and speed endurance	Harvard step test
10/10/2004	85 kg	x 5	115 kg 135%	2.09 m	6.23 m	4.7 sec	10.86 m	41	5.1 5.4 6.5 40m 80m 120m	38 pts
	kg		kg %						40m 80m 120m	
	kg		kg %						40m 80m 120m	
	kg		kg %						40m 80m 120m	
	kg		kg %						40m 80m 120m	
	kg		kg %						40m 80m 120m	
	kg		kg %						40m 80m 120m	
	kg		kg %						40m 80m 120m	
	kg		kg %						40m 80m 120m	

Strength

Please note: we will be using Olympic lifts more and more. Invest in yourself. Have your lifting technique checked by a qualified weight lifting instructor. It's your back and your career, and if you don't, and you get damaged (and you will if your technique is poor), it will be your own fault. Coaches and clubs can be found at www.bwla.com.

Work with weights a minimum of twice weekly; three times is better. *You must include a session of fast, dynamic body weight exercises – mini or standard circuit training is ideal.*

Make sure you are thoroughly warmed up before you start your weights work.

Next, work through the exercises in the sequence given below, then add *one* free-choice exercise (these are marked *); this can be any exercise you feel you need, or particularly like.

Work as follows: if you can do three sets of 10 *honest* reps, with time enough in between for your training partner to do her/his set, then the load is too light and you should raise the weight. However, if you can't do three sets of

top tip Plan your workout well in advance of your trip to the gym or track. Ideally, review the plan at least an hour or two before you even start to get your kit bag together. In this way you will have a picture in your mind of what is coming up and you will start to prepare even on the journey to where you do your training. If you can train yourself to arrive in an 'I'm on a mission' frame of mind, you will get a much more focused session than if you start by standing around deciding what to do today.

six reps then the weight is too great and you should reduce the load to ensure correct form and build up to 3 x 10.

By making every session a little different from the one before, you will avoid dulling yourself into motor stereotypes.

Abs

Continue with the exercises described in phase one and add the following exercise.

Superman

This is a progression of the plank described in phase one.

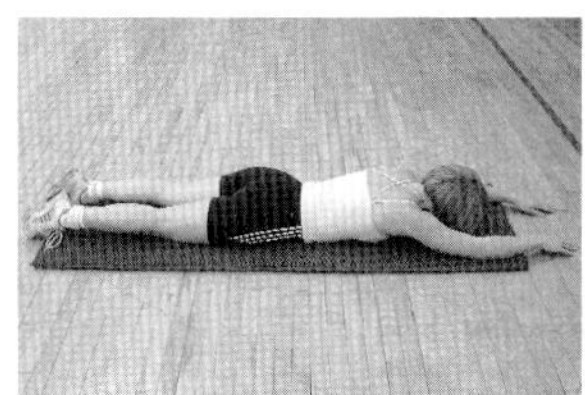
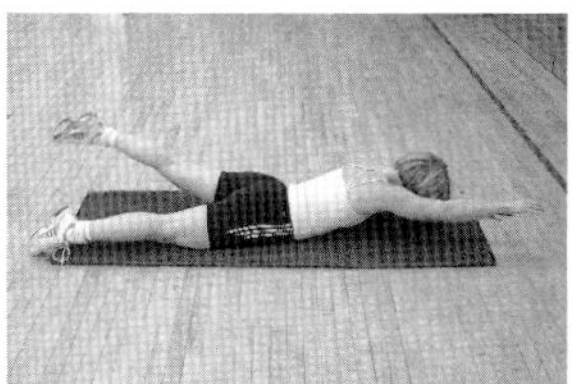

Start position
Start face down on the floor, torso and legs in a straight line

How to do it
Raise your left leg (as per the plank) and reach out with your right arm until both leg and arm are parallel with the floor

Try to keep your spine in the neutral position at all times and do not let your pelvis tilt. Concentrate on keeping your stomach in contact with the floor at all times. In this way you use the muscles of your upper back and shoulders to raise your arm, which will help overall flexibility and strength of your back. Once each side equals one repetition.

As before, you may wish to use the sample record sheet in Table 4.5 as a template that you can fill in to record your progress.

TABLE 4.5 Phase two record sheet

Phase two	Date: Reps	Weight	Date: Reps	Weight	Date: Reps	Weight	Date: Reps	Weight	Date: Reps	Weight
Power clean and jerk										
One-hand power snatch										
Squat/quarter squat										
Jump squat										
Bench press										
Upright row										
Dips										
Cheat one-hand row										
Alternate dumbbell press										
Pull-ups										
Lats and fronts										
Side bends										
Free choice										
Abs		x 7		x 8		x 9		x 10		x 11
Side		x 7		x 8		x 9		x 10		x 11

'Skipping meals will help you to lose weight ...'

In order to keep your metabolic rate (the rate at which you burn up calories) elevated, you need to eat regularly. By only eating once or twice in 24 hours, you will cause your metabolic rate to slow down and this will lead to your body holding on to its calorie reserves. In essence, your body goes into 'starvation' mode as it thinks it will not be getting any food for a while. There is also the danger that by not eating all day you will overeat or binge in the evening. People often skip breakfast in an attempt to lose weight, but after a night of not eating, breakfast is the fuel that kick-starts your metabolism, hence the saying that breakfast is the most important meal of the day.

Running work

Drills

Extend all the drills to 25 metres. After three weeks at this distance, and if you are able to complete each drill with perfect form, you can move on to the final level, which is to add ankle weights during the routines. Do not use any weights heavier than 1.5 kg; you can find these in any shop that caters for the aerobics market. When you start using ankle weights, ensure that you only train on a forgiving surface such as grass or a running track, and reduce the distance of the drills until you get the feel of them.

Speed work

If ever there was somewhere where quality must take precedence over quantity, it is here. These drills may seem to be easy and you may feel as if you are short-changing yourself. Don't worry – it's all part of the plan!

The emphasis is on top quality and top speed – you are training your body to move fast. If you overdo the quantity or underdo the rest between sets, all that you will teach your body to do is to go slow.

Take three of the drills (say, heel pick-up, knee pick-up and the bound). Set out a 20 m track. Perform the first drill for about 10 m and then explode straight into a sprint for the last 10 m.

It is ideal if you have a training partner who can shout 'Go!' at various points so, instead of anticipating the start of the sprint, you are forced to react – just as in a match situation.

To make the most efficient use of your time, you can perform drills or the speed session prior to a weights session. However, even if you do them in isolation, both of the above sessions are short and sharp, and they could be done in a lunch hour or before work.

Speed stamina

During phase two you should also include a small number of speed stamina sessions. These can be no more than 100 m at three-quarters pace with fixed recovery times that can gradually be decreased, while the number of reps is increased as you develop.

For example: 5 x 100 m @ three-quarters pace with two minutes' rest (or enough to bring your breathing back to near normal. (You may need to refer back to the previous sections on speed stamina routines.)

Next session: 5 x 100 m @ three-quarters pace with 1 minute 45 seconds' rest.

Figure 4.1 shows a record of a phase two session that a Harlequins player actually completed. It is a great illustration of the difference between phases one and two. His comment was, 'I thought phase one was hard; I didn't realise how much harder phase two was going to be.' He meant 'better' not 'harder', of course. Note his 'free choice' at the end of the session.

Note well: the sample training diaries are taken from some very experienced players. Do not *take these as a specific session for you. Remember – it is all about your progression, not what anyone else has of is doing!*

Copying someone else's routine will always be either insufficient or too hard, so you risk either wasting your time or injuring yourself!

FIGURE 4.1 Example record of a phase two session

WARM-UP:

2-mile jog, 15-min drills

LIFTS:

One-hand snatch:	4 x 32 kg left and right, 4 x 37 kg l and r, 4 x 40 kg l and r, 1 x 45 kg l and r, 1 x failed 47.5 kg	
Power clean and jerk:	4 x 60 kg, 4 x 70 kg, 4 x 80 kg, 4 x 85 kg	
Squat:	140 kg – 3 sets of 6 reps (recorded as 140 kg: 6, 6, 6)	Increase reps

EXERCISES:

Bench press:	90 kg: 10, 10, 8	Increase reps last set
One-hand row:	47.5 kg: 10, 10, 10	Hard, repeat once more
Side bends:	45, 10, 10, 10	Increase load
Dips:	body weight + 15 kg: 8, 10, 9	Increase reps last set

FREE CHOICE:

Shoulder shrugs:	145 kg: 10, 10, 10	Increase load
Trunk circuit:	12 x every exercise, non-stop, no rest between	

Phase three

Duration: do throughout August and up to the start of the season.
Aims: improvement in absolute and speed strength, power/explosive strength.

Important note

Phase three is more demanding, as it should be: you're fitter, stronger and you need a greater stimulus to create a training effect. *Be motivated!* Begin phase three with more max attempts. Go for it! Take a pride in your increasing strength. The lifts and the core exercises are still the basis for this phase, but the sessions must be more intense, more weight must be lifted and the nature of the sessions will be more explosive.

Keep training fun

During this phase you should try to set up training competitions against your team-mates. The following are examples of some highly motivating, good fun sessions. You might want to make up some more of your own, either on a team or an individual basis. The following are based on a four-players-per-team scenario.

- Each member does two sets of maximum pull-ups: the team with the highest total (or the first to finish, *while keeping form*) is the winner.
- How many bench presses using half body weight can each member do in one minute?
- What is the maximum weight that can be lifted in a 3 x 3 x 3 inclined bench press? (You can increase the weight on the bar for each set if the previous set was too easy.) The team with the highest total weight wins.
- Each member does 6 x one-hand snatch (left and right). The team with the best total weight wins a pint of beer each (or any similar reward that will act to increase motivation!).

Strength

During this phase you may need some more ideas to keep sessions new of challenging. Pyramids are a very time-efficient format while eccentric lifts provide a new training stimulus.

Pyramids

Include 'pyramids' and 'reverse pyramids' in your training. A pyramid is a series of sets, using a large number of reps at a 'light' weight to start, and ending with few reps and a much heavier load. An example is:

upright row: 10 x 20 kg, 8 x 25 kg, 6 x 30 kg, 4 x 35 kg, 2 x 40 kg, 1 x 45 kg

A reverse pyramid would be 1 x max weight (say, 70 kg), 2 x 65 kg, 4 x 60 kg, 6 x 55 kg, 8 x 50 kg.

Eccentric (or negative) lifts

These exercises definitely have no place in the beginner's programme, but if phases one and two have been diligently applied, then they are valuable. These exercises (see below) will teach your body to respond quickly immediately after working with a heavy weight. (Driving in a scrum or maul and then having to sprint to the next breakdown is a good example of how this comes in useful during a game.)

As usual, safety first and common sense to the fore please! Before you set up the exercises, think through what you will do if/when the muscle group fails.

Some examples of negative routines are the following bench press and pull-up exercises.

BENCH PRESS

Make certain your spotters are awake (you will probably need two for this exercise), know what is going on and make sure there is clear communication and prior agreement between you all. If your bench press PB is 100 kg, then load the bar to 120 kg, take off the rack and lower the bar to your chest as slowly as possible. Fight it all the way down and, if you lose it, shout 'Take!' and trust that your spotters will react quickly enough. It is quite sufficient to do two or three of these presses in a session. Follow them immediately with some light, fast reps (in this example maybe only 40 kg) or do some clap press-ups (i.e. clapping your hands with each press up from the floor).

PULL-UPS

Hang a weight disc from a weight belt worn around your waist. Stand on a stable bench in front of the pull-up bar to allow you to boost yourself up to bar level. Slowly lower yourself to full extension and then boost yourself back up to the top and repeat.

For safety, ensure that the platform or bench on which you are standing is stable and that it is under you at all times. At the point of failure you should be able to simply stand up.

LEGS

It is not advisable to try to overload your legs excessively using free weights as this will put far too much emphasis on your back. However, using machines is a safe and ideal way to isolate a muscle group and perform, say, negative hamstring curls followed by 10 tuck jumps.

Figure 4.2 shows an athlete's record of his sessions during one April week (well, just over a week). The athlete in question is coached by one of the contributors to this book.

FIGURE 4.2 Example record of one week's sessions (April)

MON:

Warm-up:	skipping	(lots)
		(plus a few warm-up sets)
Snatch:	4 x 60 kg	
	4 x 80 kg	
	4 x 100 kg	(no maxing out – really part of warm-up)
One-hand snatch:	5 x 50 kg left and right,	
	4 x 60 kg	
	3 x 70 kg	
	1 x 85 kg	(we were quite pleased with that!)
Squat:	8 x 120 kg	
	6 x 140 kg	
Squat:	4 x 160 kg	
	2 x 220 kg	
Vertical jumps:	10 x 45 kg	(high bouncing/rebounding)

Finished with coached technique session on one-hand snatch (demanding good technique when tired, to simulate need for good technique when under pressure, like competition). Walked and jogged one lap of track to cool down – included stretching, rain or no rain!

TUE:

Rugby practice:	2 hours	in the pouring rain!

20 minutes' sprinting, hopping, bouncing one- and two-footed up, down and sideways on stadium steps

Gym:	10 minutes' stretching

FIGURE 4.2 Example record – continued

WED:
Rested

THU:
Specific rugby practice: one and a half hours, very cold, went straight home!

FRI:
Rested

SAT:
Jog 2 laps of pitch, stretching

Warm-up in Gym, lots of different exercises with light weights (including one-hand snatch)

Bench:	6 x 160 kg	no rest, then
	6 x clap press-ups	
One-hand row:	8 x 60 kg	
Bench:	4 x 180 kg	no rest, then
	6 x clap press-ups	
One-hand row:	8 x 60 kg	
Bench:	1 x 200 kg	(failed number 2!)
One-hand row:	8 x 60 kg	

(The athlete was tired at this point so a break was given, water drunk and motivation applied)

Side bends:	3 x 8 x 45 kg	
Ab crunches:	15 kg held in hands close to chest,	10 left, 10 right
Chinnies:	very fast, lots of shouting, 24!	

FIGURE 4.2 Example record – continued

SUN: (evening in my garage)
Met with other players, decided on a bench press competition, warmed up with skipping, stretching and many exercises with light weights. Came in at 20 kg!! Managed 1 rep of 245 kg

MON:
Repeated a phase one session from two months ago, but missed out bench press

Abs

The exercises below can only be achieved effectively if you are comfortable with the exercises in phases one and two. Please do not be tempted to try these out until you have built your foundations by completing the earlier stages.

Remember that all exercises are started with the navel pulled towards the spine to prepare the muscle group for work.

Bench obliques

You will need a partner to hold your feet if you do not have access to a Smith machine (a Smith machine is the one with a captive barbell held in place on runners or chains).

Start position

Place a bench parallel to a Smith machine bar, and set at roughly the same height; ensure that the weight on the bar is heavy enough to trap your legs while you perform the exercise

How to do it

With your hip on the bench and lying on one side, tuck your feet under the bar; dip down with your upper body to touch the floor with your elbow; pause and then return to the starting position; one each side = 1 rep

As you tire you will tend to bend forwards and 'jack-knife' as your body tries to recruit your abdominals to help your tired obliques. Concentrate on technique and form at all times.

To progress, start with your hands by your sides and increase the weight when you are ready by putting your hands up by your ears, then by reaching out above your head to add more resistance.

After doing this for a long time you may want to add more weight. If so, simply hug a disc, but take care – these are small muscles, but if you overdo things you will put yourself out of action for a *long* time. Remember: progress slowly and consistently.

Advanced reverse crunches

You will need a partner to help you with this one.

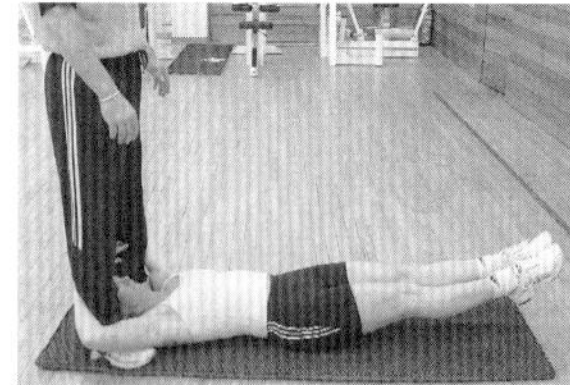
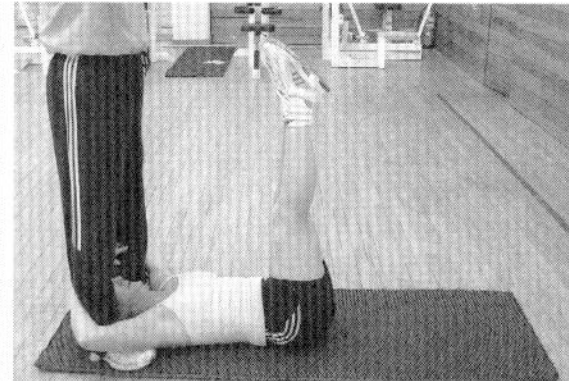

Start position

Lie flat on your back with your partner standing astride your head; take hold of his/her ankles; ask your partner to hold their hands out straight in front of them at shoulder height with their palms facing down

How to do it

Keeping your legs straight, raise your feet about 5 cm; this is your start position; now, in one smooth movement, bring your legs to a vertical position (no further); pause, and then reach up with your feet and touch your partner's hands; *slowly* and *smoothly* return to the start position

This exercise only works if you keep your legs straight and do not stray over the vertical. It is also important that you pause at each stage. By doing this, all momentum is removed from your legs and the stomach muscles have to work to raise your legs. When you first try this exercise, you will find it difficult to raise your legs vertically. The natural tendency is to let your legs go beyond the vertical towards your head – this is easier! Try not to cheat – halt at vertical and use your stomach muscles to lift. Anything other than *strict form* is a waste of time.

As a progression you can do small circuits and pyramids: reach up and touch once and then, without lowering, touch twice, three times, twice, once, and so on.

Advanced Superman

This is the same as the exercise in phase two, but this time it is done using ankle and wrist weights.

Running work

Drills

Continue with all drills at 40 m but reduce the length of your recovery periods. Ensure that proper form does not suffer; reduce your recovery time *gradually* – by perhaps only five seconds at a time.

Speed work

Here you can mix and match as you wish. However, you should take enough recovery time to ensure that only top-quality work is done at top speed. An example drill is as follows:

- drill + sprints (as per previous phase)
- hollow sprints (see previous phase)
- slaloms (keep the course short and allow plenty of recovery time).

Then gradually add the following.

DOWNHILL SPRINTS

Find a gentle slope, or run with a following wind, and use the slope/wind to assist you as you sprint. You can apply this to any of the sprint routines above. The intention is to teach your body to go faster than it would normally be able to. However, it is pointless doing assisted sets like this if your form is poor or you have not completed the previous phases and therefore do not have the proper groundwork in place.

Speed stamina

Next do some 'back to backs' (as described in the previous phases).

By now you will have no doubt started your club training nights, which means that you will have fewer opportunities to train on your own. Be aware of what the team sessions include as they may well cover some of the areas you need to include in your programme.

For example, if there is a great deal of touch rugby played in the early weeks, you can treat this as a speed session by varying the level of your involvement – go looking for the ball or cover the back line as fast as possible, and then recover by loitering on the wing for a couple of minutes.

The main thing is: whatever you don't cover in the team session needs to be dealt with in your own training. This could be managed by talking with the coach regularly to see what he is planning and, if there is likely to be a hard (and only you will know) scrummage practice, then turn up half an hour early and do your drills and speed work first.

Make the coaching team aware of what you are doing and what goals you have set yourself, and most reasonable people will be willing to help you.

5 INTERIOR DESIGN diet and nutrition

aim:

- To help you understand the key elements of nutrition and how very small changes can have a very significant impact on your preparation.

Diet as refuelling

At levels outside the top flight, diet comes lower down the list of things that can have a dramatic impact on performance – but if you wish to develop the outlook you have on your preparation for your sport, you may want to include some sensible and moderate changes to your diet.

The reason that this topic has been left until last is not because it is of least importance. It is just that it is our experience that diet is one of the hardest things to change, as it is likely to be one of your longest-standing habits. However, if you have taken the structured approach to your body conditioning that the previous chapters have suggested, then you may find yourself more open to making changes to your diet. Many athletes see diet as offering a way to enhance all their existing good work; they recognise its ability to add to, as well as detract from, all their hard work.

Although we are not suggesting you become a monk, real results can be gained by making just slight adjustments to your eating patterns. Again, it comes down to the individual: if it's important to you, you may want to make some changes, and if other things take precedence in your life then you may not. It's OK either way – just be honest with yourself.

At the risk of repeating ourselves – the most important thing, as we have seen throughout this book, is to be *honest* with yourself. If you are not, then all you are doing is setting yourself up to fail ... and you will feel guilty when you do.

By the end of this chapter you should have a general understanding of how what you put into your mouth affects your performance. The good news is that it's not rocket science. There are just some very basic rules to observe.

The basic food groups and what they do

How can you use food as a tool to improve performance?

Carbohydrate

> *Carbohydrate consumed before, during and after exercise can enhance performance.*

This is the most important nutrient for your working muscles and should make up 60–70 per cent of the energy in your diet. When eaten, carbohydrate is broken down into glucose and is then absorbed into the blood, from where it is either used as a fuel or stored as glycogen. Storage capacity, however, is limited, so a frequent supply of glucose is needed to maintain levels. Low stores will result in poor performance and an increased risk of injury.

Your requirement for carbohydrate can be calculated using the following equation:

weight (kg) x level of training = carbohydrate requirement per day

'Level of training' is classified as follows:

- light (less than one hour per day) – 4–5
- moderate (one to two hours per day) – 6–7
- heavy (more than three hours per day) – 8–10.

Therefore, the range for a 75 kg person undergoing moderate training would be 450–525 g of carbohydrate per day. The table on page 170 of the Appendix contains a list of foods and the portion sizes needed to provide 50 g of carbohydrate.

How to increase carbohydrate intake

Carbohydrate intake can be boosted by eating more:

- bread – eat plenty and, if it is fresh, cut it thicker
- rice – or other grains such as oatmeal, bulgur wheat and couscous
- fruit – as part of a meal, as a snack or added to dishes
- pasta – or noodles
- cereals – can be eaten at any time of day
- veg – fresh, frozen or canned (e.g. baked beans, chickpeas, kidney beans).

Other ideas to increase carbohydrate intake include:

- snacking on high-carbohydrate foods
- eating sugary foods that are energy-dense
- using high-carbohydrate drinks (e.g. fruit juice, soft drinks, low-fat milkshakes, sports drinks).

Protein

Protein is used to replace cells and build new tissue. That's why it's essential for maintaining and building muscle mass. However, there is no evidence that a high protein intake enhances metabolic efficiency or increases muscle bulk, so high-protein diets are simply a waste of money! Current evidence does suggest, however, that protein requirements are increased as a result of strength, speed and endurance training, so an active person will need more than a sedentary Joe. Remember, though, that any protein consumed in excess of requirements is converted by the body into energy or, more likely, stored by the body as fat.

The amount of protein in an adult's diet should be in the range of 1.2–1.7 g/kg per day. Therefore, for a 75 kg player, the amount of protein in the diet should be between 90 and 128 g per day.

Including a variety of protein-rich foods in your diet will increase your protein intake. However, a lot of these foods may also be high in fat, so make wise choices. The table on page 171 of the Appendix contains a list of foods and the portion sizes needed to provide 10 g of protein.

Fat

Fat is a concentrated form of energy. It provides twice the number of calories as the same weight of protein or carbohydrate. All fat, whether butter, margarine, olive oil or the fat on your kebab meat, has the same number of calories for a given weight, and too much fat in your diet, especially too much saturated fat, can lead to health problems such as heart disease. High-fat diets also contain high levels of cholesterol, which is problematic in high quantities. Fat is, however, essential in the diet because it acts as a carrier for the fat-soluble vitamins (A, D, E and K). It should not, though, make up any more than 20 per cent of your energy intake. Unlike carbohydrate, which can only be stored in limited amounts, there is always sufficient fat available as fuel for exercise and even the leanest of competitors has a large reserve of fat for energy.

Here are some simple methods that can help you to reduce the fat content of your diet.

- Cut out margarine and butter, which are virtually all fat, and replace them with jam or honey, which contain virtually no fat.
- Eat low-fat dairy products (cheese and yoghurts) instead of full-fat products.

- Grill, poach, bake, steam, microwave or casserole food instead of frying it.
- If frying food, use an oil-substitute spray instead of adding fat.
- Choose lean cuts of meat, cut off any visible fat and skim off visible fat when cooking.
- Remove the skin from poultry.
- Keep your intake of pastry products to a minimum.
- If you eat chips, choose thick-cut over French fries, and oven chips over fried chips.
- Fill jacket potatoes with moist fillings such as beans instead of butter, margarine and cheese.
- Make custards and sauces with low-fat milk.
- Choose reduced-fat versions of muffins, cakes, puddings and so on.

If you are serious about reducing your fat intake, you should also learn to read food labels because '95 per cent fat free' does not necessarily mean that only 5 per cent of the calories come from fat! Companies want to sell products and what better way to do so than to say they are good for you? However, there are easy ways to see through these claims.

First, read the ingredient list on the label. Ingredients are listed in descending order. If fat is in the top three or listed several times by various names, then the food is probably high in fat. Fats may be hidden under the following aliases: vegetable fat, vegetable oil, animal fat, shortening, lard, cream, butter or margarine.

Second, if you are very serious, look for the fat content by weight of the food and work out the percentage of fat in the food. Nutritional information is listed on the packaging. A food label may say that there is 10 g of fat in 100 g of a product – *great*, less than 20 per cent fat! Or is it? Remember that fat contains 9 kcal per gram as opposed to the 4 kcal per gram in carbohydrate and protein. Therefore, to work out the true percentage of fat in a food you need to multiply the number of grams of fat per 100 g by nine and then find out what percentage this represents of the number of calories per 100 g. Confused? Try the following example.

Whole milk
The label says:

- 4 g fat per 100 ml
- 69 kcal per 100 ml

The calculations are as follows:

4 g x 9 kcal = 36 kcal from fat in 100 ml
36 kcal/69 kcal = 52 per cent fat .

So, whole milk that seemed quite low in fat at first glance is in fact *52 per cent fat*!

The moral of this story is: do not believe everything you read on the packet.

Vitamins and minerals

Vitamins and minerals are essential in your diet, but do you need to become a walking pillbox to get enough? The simple answer is no. If you are eating a well-balanced diet that includes foods from all of the main food groups (fruit and veg, breads and cereals, dairy products, meat and fish or alternatives), you are unlikely to be deficient in vitamins or minerals. Taking vitamin and mineral supplements is not necessary if you do not have any proven deficiencies. If, however, you do decide to take a supplement, please heed the following advice.

- Check with your chemist that you have chosen a suitable supplement.
- Check that it will not interfere with any other supplements or medication that you take.
- Follow the manufacturer's dosage instructions – do not double the dose for luck!
- Remember that 'mega' doses of vitamins or minerals, or taking large doses of single vitamins or minerals, can be harmful to your health and will not improve performance.

Eating to lose weight (fat)

The secret to losing fat mass is calories: if you're eating too many and/or not 'burning' enough off, it is impossible to lose fat.

To lose fat you need to create an energy deficit either through decreasing your energy intake or increasing your energy expenditure; a combination of the two is best. However, if you are already pretty active it may be difficult to further increase your energy expenditure, so decreasing your energy intake may be the best path for you. The reduction in your energy intake should not be so large as to affect your health or performance; most people need to subtract 500–800 calories from their energy intake in order to lose weight.

Losing fat, not muscle

The goal is to lose fat, not lean body mass (muscle). Ideally, your body fat should be monitored throughout the period of weight loss. If fat mass loss does not equate with weight loss then it is possible that you are losing lean body mass, which is not good for performance. This may happen if energy restrictions are too high and weight loss occurs too rapidly. If you find you are losing lean body mass, you may need to adjust your dietary plan.

Rate of loss

Safe and effective weight loss should not exceed 2 lb (about 1 kg) per week. If you are losing more than this, it is again likely that you are losing lean body mass (see above). Initially, the rate of weight loss will be high and may represent more than 1 kg a week. However, as time passes the rate will gradually decrease and may represent half a pound per week or less after several months.

Energy intake breakdown

Your weight loss diet should be made up of approximately 60–70 per cent carbohydrate, 10–20 per cent protein and less than 20 per cent fat. The recommended carbohydrate intake is similar to that for optimal training and so should not hinder your performance; remember that a high carbohydrate intake is needed for hard training. Carbohydrate is also protein-sparing (it prevents muscles being broken down for energy) and, contrary to popular opinion, it is not fattening. Low-carbohydrate diets will only lead to lowered carbohydrate stores, poor performance and muscle breakdown.

If some 10–20 per cent of your intake comes from protein, this will provide your body with sufficient protein to maintain muscle mass without you being at risk of consuming an excess that will be stored as fat. Fat intake should make up less than 20 per cent of your total calories; excess fat will also be stored as body fat. However, it is not necessary to drop below 10 per cent fat, and cutting all fat from your diet can actually slow muscle growth, decrease strength and decrease energy levels. A low-fat diet is much better for weight loss than a non-fat diet.

You should try to combine carbohydrate and protein at each meal. Eating carbohydrate by itself causes a rapid rise in blood sugar and insulin. This promotes fat storage and causes 'rebound hypoglycaemia' (low blood sugar), leading to hunger pangs – not good if you're trying to lose weight! By combining foods properly, you can control your blood sugar and insulin, keep your energy levels steady and enhance muscle gain, while minimising fat storage.

Quality versus quantity

Fat-loss programmes are not 'starvation diets' or excuses to eat a small amount of rubbish! Losing fat mass without losing muscle mass is possible, but only if you consume a sensible amount of quality calories. Your diet should include foods from every food group: grains/cereals, veg, fruit, dairy products, meat and fish. Good sources of carbohydrate include rice, potatoes, beans, pasta, breakfast cereals and bread. Good sources of protein include low-fat dairy products, chicken, turkey, fish and lean red meat.

Eating to gain weight (muscle)

Once again, the secret to gaining body mass is calories – if you're not eating enough it is impossible to gain muscle!

In order to gain mass you need to eat more calories than you are 'burning', but that doesn't mean you can go and live at McDonald's! Most people will need to eat an extra 300–500 kcal per day to gain weight. To be more precise, you should add 2 kcal per pound of body mass (1 kg = 2.2 lb) on to your daily energy intake.

Gaining muscle, not fat

The goal here is to gain lean muscle mass, not fat. Body fat should, again, be monitored and if your body fat increases you can try adding 20–30 minutes of aerobic work to your workout three or four days a week. If your body fat still increases you can try 'zig-zagging' your calorie intake. This means three days where you consume your additional calories for weight gain followed by three days where you don't. This should allow lean mass gain without an increase in body fat.

Rate of gain

You should expect maximum increases of half to one pound per week (slightly less for females). If, in two weeks, you haven't gained any weight, you probably aren't eating enough and should make an attempt to increase your energy intake. After three to four months, the rate will slow down and may only be around a quarter of a pound per week.

Energy intake ratios

The ideal ratios for weight gain are approximately 55–65 per cent carbohydrate, 20–30 per cent protein and 10–20 per cent fat. Although the recommended carbohydrate intake is lower than that for optimal training, it should still make up the bulk of your calories. Your protein intake may need to increase (increased protein intake is needed for muscular gain). As with weight loss, a low-fat diet is much better for muscle growth than a non-fat diet.

Small, frequent meals

The best way to eat when trying to gain weight is to eat five or six meals a day, spaced two and a half to three hours apart. The main reason for this is that the amount of calories you would have to eat per meal in just three meals would probably be too much for your body to process at one sitting. More is not necessarily better: your body can only process so many calories at once and, remember, excess calories will be converted to fat.

Eating small, frequent meals also promotes better muscle growth as it helps regulate insulin levels. Insulin aids the transport of amino acids, the building blocks for muscles, into the muscle itself and is a very powerful growth-promoting hormone. By eating smaller, more frequent meals you maintain a steady level of insulin, enabling it to perform its growth-promoting role more effectively. It also prevents the breakdown of muscle that can occur if you go a long time without eating. If you don't eat protein at regular intervals, your body begins to break down its own muscle to serve its amino acid needs. Amino acids can't be stored in the body and are only 'useful' for about three hours after the ingestion of protein. So it is advisable to eat a meal containing protein every three hours. However, eating more protein than you need will not help, as your body can only use so much protein at any one time. At best, any excess will be wasted; at worst, it will be converted into body fat.

If it is difficult to consume five or six meals a day (perhaps while you are out at work, for example), you might find that it is worth replacing one or two meals a day with meal-replacement drinks. However, take care when choosing these as commercially available products are often about 80 per cent sugar and contain very little protein. Ideally, you need a product with a ratio of one part protein to two parts carbohydrate. Alternatively, you could take a low-calorie meal replacement product and mix it with milk or juice, and blend in some fresh fruit to create a high-protein, weight-gain shake. Remember, though, that meal replacements should be used for convenience only; they are not designed to replace food completely and they are in no way better than food.

Eating and competition

Before matches/training

After a good kip, your carbohydrate stores will be almost drained and you will be fairly dehydrated, unless you are prone to indulging in midnight feasts! You need to account for these factors before training and matches.

A high-carbohydrate meal – which is also low in fat, fibre and bulk – three hours before matches and training, is recommended. This will enhance performance by increasing the amount of carbohydrate available late in the exercise session (i.e. towards the end of the half when you are flagging). However, if you cannot eat three hours before exercise, due to early-morning training or nerves, remember that something is better than nothing. Try to eat a high-carbohydrate snack such as a bowl of cereal, some toast and jam, a cereal bar or some fruit. Alternatively, have a carbohydrate drink instead of anything solid.

It is important that you also ensure you are fully hydrated prior to exercise. Beginning exercise in a dehydrated state will impair your performance. As a general rule you should try to consume a pint of fluid (not lager!) before going to bed and a pint on waking. You should then top this up at a rate of one pint per hour up until one hour pre-exercise. Finally, 20 minutes before you start playing or training you should try to consume another half pint.

During matches/training

Prolonged exercise challenges our carbohydrate stores and our ability to regulate body temperature. Ingesting a carbohydrate–electrolyte drink, of appropriate concentration, during training and competing will help to address these limiting factors.

Ingesting carbohydrate during exercise increases blood glucose availability and uptake by the working muscles. This increases the use of glucose as an energy source, as opposed to muscle glycogen (stored carbohydrate), and creates a 'glycogen-sparing' effect. This results in more carbohydrate being available later on in the match or session, and maintains your ability to use carbohydrate as a fuel. This helps prevent physical and mental fatigue.

Some 30–60 g of carbohydrate, or 600–1200 ml of isotonic carbohydrate–electrolyte drink per hour of exercise is recommended. This is a fairly large volume of fluid, so it is best to drink it in smaller volumes (150–300 ml) at regular intervals (every 15–20 minutes). If carbohydrate drinks are not available, drink the same volume of water, diluted fruit juice or squash.

Post-match/training

Following prolonged activity, your carbohydrate stores will need refilling and you will need to replace any fluids you have lost. Performance is only reproducible if you do so. You should start to replace the energy used immediately after the match/session. Waiting, even for 30 minutes, wastes valuable time that could be being used to ensure that your next training session or match is not below par.

The following guidelines are useful for post-exercise energy intake.

- Consume 50 g carbohydrate *as soon as possible* in liquid form (1 litre of 6 per cent isotonic drink) or as easily digestible carbohydrate (dried fruit, sugar-based sweets).
- Your first meal after exercise should be high in carbohydrate and low in fat.
- Aim to consume 10 g carbohydrate per kg body weight in the first 24 hours of recovery.
- If it is not possible to consume this amount as solid carbohydrate, top it up with carbohydrate drinks.

Rehydration is as important as consuming enough carbohydrate. To achieve full rehydration, you will need to consume 150–200 per cent of the fluid lost during exercise. For example, someone losing 2 kg of body mass during exercise will need to consume three to four litres of fluid to rehydrate themselves completely. Drinking plain water is not as beneficial as drinking fluid with added sodium as this will prevent increased urine production, stimulate thirst and improve absorption. Isotonic carbohydrate drinks are ideal for use after exercise. However, do not consume drinks that contain caffeine (i.e. Coke). Caffeine is a diuretic and will cause further water loss through urination, and therefore further dehydration.

To sum up ...

Before matches/training

- Consume 600 ml (one pint) fluid before you go to bed and 600 ml when you get up.

- Consume a high-carbohydrate meal three hours before exercise.
- Consume 600 ml of fluid per hour prior to exercise.
- Consume 250–500 ml of fluid 20 minutes before exercise.

During matches/training

- Consume 30–60 g carbohydrate per hour.

Recovery from matches/training

- Consume 50 g carbohydrate as soon as possible post-exercise; continue this intake hourly up until the first solid meal.
- The first meal should contain 1–1.5 g/kg carbohydrate.
- Consume 10 g/kg carbohydrate in the first 24 hours of recovery.
- Consume 150–200 per cent of fluid lost in order to rehydrate fully.

Fluid

Fluid is possibly the most important and most commonly overlooked dietary component. Water is very important to the effective operation of your body, and even small reductions in body water (dehydration) will dramatically and quickly affect performance and, in severe cases, endanger life.

Fluid is needed to:

- avoid dehydration and the reduction in performance associated with it
- regulate body temperature
- maintain the function of virtually all the cells in the human body
- lubricate joints and eyes
- get rid of waste products from the body.

It is essential that you consume adequate fluid on a daily basis – not just when you are training or playing, although you will need to increase the amount you take in at these times. A good daily intake is important as it teaches your body to tolerate and absorb larger amounts of fluid, which means that you will not feel uncomfortably bloated during training and matches. As for training to 'tolerate dehydration' – you can't. This is like saying that a car can learn to tolerate an empty radiator – it is absolute codswallop!

Another commonly held myth, as we have already seen, is that 'sweating will help you lose weight' – rubbish, again! People who train in waterproofs (or even bin bags) in an attempt to lose weight may as well kiss goodbye to optimal performance. Although this practice probably results in instant weight loss, the weight will be replaced as soon as rehydration takes place. However, if those who try this regime fail to rehydrate so as to maintain their weight loss, they will find themselves having to cope with the effects of dehydration, which will be a lot more harmful to them and their performance than a little extra weight could ever be.

The effects of dehydration

During all types of activity, heat is produced and lost from the body via sweat. Hard exercise may require up to one litre per hour of fluid intake; however, few players will meet these demands. This is especially worrying when you consider that performance can be significantly impaired by as little as 2 per cent dehydration, and the greater the loss of body water, the more pronounced the reduction in performance (a loss of 5 per cent of body mass can decrease performance by 30 per cent).

Recent studies have shown that there is no critical point of dehydration at which performance becomes impaired. Instead, there is a gradual erosion of performance as the degree of dehydration increases. Heart rate rises, you feel that you are working harder and body temperature regulation becomes more difficult with every percentage of water loss. But the effects creep up on you, so you may not even notice it happening until it's too late!

How much water do you need?

The amount lost through breathing, sweating and excretion varies from person to person and depends on age, climate, diet and the amount of exercise you do. However, the average man should consume at least 2.9 litres (6 pints) of water per day and the average women at least 2 litres (4.5 pints) per day. Some of this will be in the food you eat, so aiming for 1.5–2 litres of liquid per day should be adequate for the average, sedentary person. You will then need extra fluid to cover any activity you do, such as training and playing.

Weight as an indicator of fluid loss

Using weight as an indicator of fluid loss is very useful. By weighing yourself immediately before and after training/matches, you can estimate how much fluid you have lost (as you lose fluid from your body you lose weight).

- One kilo of weight loss equals one litre (1.75 pints) of fluid loss – this needs to be replaced *as soon as possible* after exercise.
- If you have lost fluid, consuming the same amount as was lost will not rehydrate you; you will need to consume 150–200 per cent of the amount lost in order to fully account for it. This is because over the next few hours you will still be losing fluid by continuing to sweat and through urinating, so simply drinking the amount that was lost will not do.
- Try to standardise weighing conditions; your scales should be on the same level surface each time you weigh yourself to ensure that you get accurate and consistent readings.
- Weigh yourself in minimal clothing, and towel off beforehand – being wet will artificially increase your weight, especially if you are wearing sweat- or water-soaked clothes.

When to drink

It is not just a case of drinking when you become thirsty, as thirst is a poor indicator of fluid needs. Indeed, if you wait until you are thirsty, this will probably mean that you are already dehydrated and your performance will be affected despite any intake of fluid.

> *Ideally, during training and matches, you should drink every 15–20 minutes to remain fully hydrated (i.e. to make sure you have enough water in your body).*

Water, however, may not be the ideal solution for fluid replacement during exercise; isotonic carbohydrate drinks are better. They not only help you to avoid dehydration, but also to maintain the availability of carbohydrate, which is the body's fuel.

TABLE 5.1 Symptoms of dehydration (as a percentage of body weight loss)

% body weight loss	Symptoms
0.5	Thirst
2	Stronger thirst, discomfort, appetite loss
3	Dry mouth, reduced, darkened urine
4	Increased effort, flushed skin, impatience, apathy
5	Difficulty concentrating
6	Impaired temperature regulation
8	Dizziness, laboured breathing, confusion
10	Spasticity, imbalance, swollen tongue, delirium
11	Kidney failure, circulatory insufficiency

DIY sports drinks

Well-formulated sports drinks contain the correct amounts of carbohydrate and electrolytes (sodium and potassium; don't worry about the chemistry, just trust us – they are important) to maximise the absorption of the drink and provide the body with sufficient fluid and carbohydrate to optimise performance.

Commercially available drinks are fine, but can be expensive. You can make your own using the following recipes. It is difficult to recreate commercial sports drinks accurately, so it is essential you measure the ingredients you are using carefully so that the composition of the drink is correct.

Different drinks are suitable for different conditions, as described below.

For normal training and playing conditions

These are called 'isotonic drinks' and are 6–7 per cent carbohydrate.

- 50–70 g sugar
- 1 litre warm water

- 1–1.5 g salt
- sugar-free squash for flavour

or

- 200 ml ordinary fruit squash
- 800 ml water
- 1–1.5 g salt

or

- 500 ml unsweetened fruit juice
- 500 ml water
- 1–1.5 g salt

When playing or training conditions are hotter than normal

These are called 'hypotonic drinks' and are 2–3 per cent carbohydrate.

- 20–30 g sugar
- 1 litre warm water
- 1–1.5 g salt
- sugar-free squash for flavour

or

- 100 ml ordinary fruit squash
- 900 ml water
- 1–1.5 g salt

or

- 250 ml unsweetened fruit juice
- 750 ml water
- 1–1.5 g salt

To sum up ...

- Fluid consumption is vital during training and matches as well as at rest.
- Form a plan for fluid intake. Don't leave it to chance – always take a full drinks bottle to training and matches.
- Always start training/matches well hydrated, and drink little and often throughout.
- Remember, thirst is a poor indicator of fluid needs – drink *before* you get thirsty.
- Drink during scheduled breaks in training/matches or in ad hoc breaks (e.g. when there are stoppages for injuries or penalties).
- Practise drinking during training – never try a new drink or drinking strategy during a match.
- Choose a drink you like the taste of and can afford.
- Fully rehydrate between training sessions and matches.
- Remember your dental health too – sports drinks contain sugar and can contribute to tooth decay. (For this reason never drink anything other than water after you clean your teeth at night. Even the weakest drink or milk will promote decay while you sleep.)
- Monitoring morning body weight is a good way to pick up on chronic dehydration.

Alcohol

The typical post-match diet will invariably include alcohol at some point. The issue with alcohol is how to ensure that it has as small an impact as possible on your subsequent training and matches. Most nutrition-related textbooks will warn you off alcohol but, in reality, most sports people will have a drink or two (or maybe ten) at some point during the week – it's how you cope with it that is the important factor.

The post-match pub visit is customary in many teams, but there are ways in which you can limit the effects of alcohol on your subsequent training and performance. After matches/training your alcohol intake should not interfere with your rehydration and refuelling needs.

- Remember that alcohol is not good for replacing the fluid lost from the body during a match or training. In fact, it is a diuretic (it makes you lose water) and will serve to dehydrate you further.
- Regardless of what the urban myth says, alcohol is not a way to 'carbo-load' or refuel, and alcoholic drinks will not contribute to your carbohydrate stores – they may even impair glycogen synthesis and so reduce energy levels. The calories in alcoholic drinks come from the alcohol itself, not from carbohydrate.

However, even if you have rehydrated and refuelled, there is another reason why you should think carefully about the amount you drink after a match. Alcohol has a vasodilatory effect (it widens blood vessels) and this can cause extra swelling and bleeding in any damaged tissue. This will delay recovery and may also cause further damage to the injured area. For injured players, the most sensible thing to do is to avoid alcohol for 24 to 48 hours and celebrate (or commiserate) a day or two late.

How harmful is the occasional drinking binge?

You are not going to like this ...

Unfortunately, even a single drinking session will cause some sort of damage. As explained above, it will delay recovery; in addition to this, it will cause impairment of the following factors (and these effects may last up to 14 hours):

- balance
- reaction time
- co-ordination
- skill performance
- mental capacity.

Add this to the headaches, nausea, fatigue and dehydration associated with a hangover and this could crucially affect your next match/training session.

Another factor to take into account, if body weight is an issue for you, is that alcohol has around 7 kcal/g and is therefore quite energy-dense. So, a good night out can add thousands of calories to your energy intake, and that's before we take into account the kebabs and curries.

The following list defines the body's reactions to alcohol.

- After just a couple of drinks the appetite is stimulated because alcohol triggers an increase in the gastric juices in the stomach.
- This fools the stomach into thinking that food is on its way when it isn't.
- This leads to hunger pangs – staunched, perhaps, with a few packets of crisps.
- After three to five drinks, the hunger wears off as the sugar content of the alcohol causes blood sugar levels to even out, reducing the craving for food.
- Additionally, the calories in the alcohol supply fuel, further reducing hunger pangs.
- However, after five or more drinks, an overload in sugar from the alcohol makes the body produce insulin, which results in a crash in blood sugar levels.
- Consequently, the cravings return even more intensely and if you don't eat at this stage you will begin to get irritable and angry. This is the point where anything you eat will taste good ... even that dodgy kebab!

The table on page 169 of the Appendix details the calorific content of some common alcoholic drinks.

How to improve your diet without becoming a monk

OK, so we've given you the bad news, and you've found out that your diet is a closer match to that of the late Oliver Reed (before he passed away, of course) than a finely tuned athlete. What can you *realistically* do about it, remembering that you will not always have access to, or the desire for, steamed fish and broccoli for every meal? Well, if you are in need of some suggestions, here they are.

Easy ways to cut calories and fat

Or 'How to cut 100 calories from your diet without really trying'.

Each of the suggestions in Table 5.2 will enable you to cut at least 100 calories out of your diet.

Fast food and fitness

Nobody playing outside the professional ranks is likely to avoid the odd slip. This book is about balance, so it will be useful for you to know what you can eat that won't wreck the hard training you have done.

You will notice that we haven't included the well-known burger and chicken outlets in the following pages – if you want to know about them, why not take a look at Table A.4 in the Appendix to see what wholesome effect (not!) they are likely to have on you.

General tips

Here are some guidelines to follow when eating out. The key here is just to understand the principles and be moderate in your choices.

- Choose meals that aren't fried – ask for grilled meat and/or fish.
- Choose tomato-based sauces not cream-based ones.
- Choose jacket potatoes or boiled potatoes as an alternative to chips or sauté potatoes.
- Eat plenty of salad, vegetables and fruit.

TABLE 5.2 Calorie-cutting changes

Change from	Change to
Sugar-free muesli, whole milk (250 kcal)	All-Bran, semi-skimmed milk (150 kcal)
2 scrambled eggs, milk and butter (296 kcal)	2 poached eggs (147 kcal)
2 grilled pork sausages (254 kcal)	2 grilled rashers of lean bacon (146 kcal)
1 freshly baked croissant (216 kcal)	2 slices of toast from a small loaf (116 kcal)
2 pats of real butter (144 kcal)	2 tbsps of raspberry jam (42 kcal)
150 g of Greek yoghurt (240 kcal)	150 g low-fat plain yoghurt (84 kcal)
1 beef and horseradish sandwich (347 kcal)	1 lean ham and mustard sandwich (243 kcal)
1 egg mayonnaise sandwich (641 kcal)	1 egg salad sandwich (401 kcal)
1 bowl of cream of tomato soup (165 kcal)	1 bowl of gazpacho (60 kcal)
1 baked potato, butter and cheese (409 kcal)	1 baked potato with baked beans (265 kcal)
1 rounded tbsp of mayonnaise (139 kcal)	1 tbsp of salsa (20 kcal)
2 fresh bagels (402 kcal)	2 fresh wholemeal rolls (230 kcal)
1 portion of spaghetti carbonara (539 kcal)	1 portion of spaghetti Neapolitan (339 kcal)
150 g of chip-shop chips (358 kcal)	150 g of supermarket oven chips (250 kcal)
2 grilled lamb chops (664 kcal)	8 oz grilled rump steak (436 kcal)
1 chicken breast with skin (302 kcal)	1 lean turkey breast (194 kcal)
1 plate of chicken korma (660 kcal)	1 plate of chicken piri-piri (375 kcal)
1 steamed salmon steak (360 kcal)	2 grilled fishcakes (197 kcal)
1 Mars bar (287 kcal)	1 Flake bar (180 kcal)
3 chocolate digestive biscuits (222 kcal)	3 Jaffa Cakes (109 kcal)
50 g bag of salted peanuts (301 kcal)	50 g of Twiglets (192 kcal)
4 fresh figs (167 kcal)	20 fresh cherries (38 kcal)
2 bananas, small bunch of grapes (155 kcal)	1 slice of melon, 1 kiwi (49 kcal)
1 Magnum ice cream (287 kcal)	1 Solero ice cream (125 kcal)
3 cups of tea, sugar and semi-skimmed milk (158 kcal)	3 cups of tea, no sugar, skimmed milk (40 kcal)
1 glass of Baileys Irish Cream (150 kcal)	1 glass of Scotch whisky (50 kcal)
300 ml glass of whole milk (204 kcal)	300 ml glass of semi-skimmed milk (102 kcal)
1 can of Coca-Cola (128 kcal)	1 can of Diet Coca-Cola (2 kcal)
1 mug of drinking chocolate with semi-skimmed milk (178 kcal)	1 cup of Options hot chocolate with water (40 kcal)
half pint of vintage cider (286 kcal)	half pint of Guinness (105 kcal)

- Try to eat high-carbohydrate food choices such as pasta, rice or pizza (deep pan) instead of high-fat foods, and have extra bread with your meal.
- Choose desserts such as fruit, low-fat ice cream, sorbets, yoghurt and fromage frais.

Indian food

LOWER FAT

- **Starters**

  Tikka or tandoori, shish kebab, tandoori grill, dokhala (daal), Bombay mix, poppadoms and chutneys

- **Main courses**

  Dupiaza, bhuna, jalfrezi, rogan josh, dhansak, original balti sauces or tandoori kebabs, biryani, thali

- **Side orders**

  Aloo gobi, Bombay potatoes, pnar and spinach, daal, raitha, tarka daal (lentil sauce), bhindi, channa (chickpeas) and saag (spinach); boiled, basmati and mushroom rice dishes; original naan and chapatti breads

- **Desserts**

  Fresh fruit, sorbet, ice cream, lassi and kulfi

HIGHER FAT

- **Starters**

  Samosas, bhajis, aloo vadhal, crispy rolls, pakora, curry patties, wada and prawn puri

- **Main courses**

  Masala, korma and pasanda dishes

- **Side orders**

  Daal masala, pakoras, bhajis, special fried rice, egg fried rice, keema rice; keema, peshwari and garlic naans, paratha and puri (fried) breads

- **Desserts**

  Apple and banana fritters, kheer and jallebi

Mexican

LOWER FAT

- **Starters**

  Bean soup, buffalo wings, guacamole dip and taco salad

- **Main courses**

  Burritos, enchiladas, fajitas, tacos, chili con carne, kebabs, paella

- **Side orders**

  Jacket potatoes, corn tortillas, rice, guacamole and salad

- **Desserts**

  Fresh fruit, ice cream, sorbets

HIGHER FAT

- **Starters**

  Nachos with cheese, stuffed garlic mushrooms, deep-fried potato skins

- **Main courses**

  Chimichangas, hamburgers, fries

- **Side orders**

  French fries, fried onions, fried mushrooms, garlic bread with cheese, refried beans, salad dressings, sour cream

- **Desserts**

  Cheesecake, pecan pie etc. with cream

Italian

LOWER FAT

- **Starters**

  Bread sticks, ciabatta, focaccia, corn on the cob, vegetable or minestrone soup, pâté with toast, parma ham with melon, meatballs in tomato sauce

- **Main courses**

  Napolitana, bolognese, pizzaiola, puttanesca, primavera, vongole, funghi, prosciutto, all'arrabbiata and provencale sauces, pizza (deep pan)

- **Desserts**

  Fresh fruit salad, ice cream, sorbet, pancakes with fruit, cheese and biscuits

HIGHER FAT

- **Starters**

  Deep-fried whitebait or squid, garlic mushrooms, garlic bread

- **Main courses**

  Carbonara, gamberetti and any other creamy sauces

- **Desserts**

  Tiramisu, Italian gateau, zabaglione, cheesecake

Chinese

LOWER FAT

- **Starters**

  Soups, meat or fish satay dip, aromatic duck with pancakes, lettuce wraps, prawn crackers

- **Main courses**

  Chow mein, chop suey or foo yung dishes, bean sprout, chilli, oyster, yellow, sweet and sour or black bean sauces, curries

- **Side orders**

  Stir-fried Chinese veg, noodles and salads, boiled rice

- **Desserts**

  Fresh fruit, lychees, sorbet, ice cream, toffee banana/apple

HIGHER FAT

- **Starters**

  Spare ribs, spring rolls, sesame prawn toast, crispy seaweed, fried bean curd

- **Main courses**

  Food served in batter, satay sauce, fried rice

- **Side orders**

  Fried veg, battered veg, special fried rice, prawn fried rice

- **Desserts**

  Apple, banana and pineapple fritters

Wonder supplements

You must make up your own mind about supplements, but you'll get most of what you want from a proper balanced diet.

There are plenty of super-duper supplements available on the market that make all sorts of spurious claims. We recommend that you follow the rule 'If it's too good to be true, it probably is.' There are times and instances when it may be appropriate to use a supplement, but don't fall into the trap of believing that they can take the place of proper physical preparation.

Stirring creatine powder into your third pint of lager after a training session really isn't going to have any positive effect. If you are honest with yourself and you have read the previous pages, you will know what *will* make a change and what is just 'window dressing'. However, described below are a few of the more regularly used supplements and a little bit about them.

Creatine

Scientific evidence suggests that short-term creatine supplementation can improve performance during repeated high-intensity exercise; therefore, it seems that it should be beneficial for rugby performance. Creatine is possibly the only 'effective' ergogenic aid that does not contravene International Olympic Committee (IOC) doping regulations and, as such, it would be inappropriate not to make its use an option to those athletes that may find it beneficial.

Current scientific thinking views short-term creatine supplementation as a safe, effective and legal ergogenic aid. However, recent reports (highlighted in the media) have questioned both the safety and ethics of its use. These issues are discussed below to enable you to make an informed decision regarding its use.

What is it?

Here comes the science part ...

Creatine is a naturally occurring, nitrogenous, organic compound that is made in the body from certain amino acids (the building blocks of protein, as we have seen). It is then transported via the blood to sites (primarily skeletal muscle) where it is stored as phosphocreatine. In addition to the creatine that is made in the body, creatine is also eaten in the diet (primarily in the form of meat and fish). One kilo of raw steak contains about 4 g of creatine; however, some of this will be destroyed when it is cooked. The estimated daily need for creatine in humans is about 2 g, although there is no recommended dietary allowance (RDA). It is estimated that, of these 2 g, 1 g is eaten and 1 g is made by the body.

What does it do?

Oh dear – more science ...

Energy for muscle action is supplied by a substance called adenosine triphosphate (ATP). When ATP is broken down, energy is released. However, muscles can only store enough ATP to perform high-intensity muscle actions for about 10 seconds, and they will fatigue if ATP levels drop below 25–30 per cent of the normal level. So, you need to maintain ATP levels if you want to continue to exercise at the same intensity.

Phosphocreatine can be broken down quickly to provide a source of creatine and phosphate and, as such, acts as a reserve of high-energy phosphates. These phosphates are used to form more ATP. Therefore, the ability to supply ATP and delay the onset of fatigue depends on the stores of phosphocreatine in the muscles. The breakdown of phosphocreatine creates ATP very quickly. It is also very sensitive to slight drops in ATP levels, which is why it is the main source of energy at the start of high-intensity exercise when the demand for ATP is strong.

The theory behind supplementing with creatine is that it increases the availability of phosphocreatine in the muscles, which may enhance energy provision during brief, high-intensity exercise. It may also increase the phosphocreatine stores within muscles, allowing a faster rate of ATP regeneration both during and after high-intensity exercise. Effective supplementation can increase muscle creatine levels by a maximum of 20–40 per cent, but this depends on the individual. There seem to be 'responders' and 'non-responders', and there is no sure-fire way of identifying who will respond.

Research has shown that greater concentrations of phosphocreatine lead to better maintenance of ATP concentrations during single maximal sprints, and increased ATP and phosphocreatine regeneration following an intense sprint, therefore increasing the amount of work that can be performed during subsequent sprints. Creatine supplementation may also elevate gains in muscle mass when combined with weight training due to the fact that more work can be done at a higher intensity.

The argument for

Scientific evidence suggests that short-term creatine supplementation can improve performance during repeated high-intensity exercise. Current thinking views short-term supplementation as a safe, effective and legal aid to performance.

In the early 1990s, research began into the impact of creatine supplementation on exercise performance. Since then, the amount of research on creatine has ballooned, with some positive and some negative findings. Some of the studies that have shown a beneficial effect are outlined below.

- Mujika (2000) studied the effects of creatine on intermittent, high-intensity exercise specific to competitive soccer, and found that repeated sprint performance was enhanced after supplementation.
- Stone (1999) supplemented American football players with creatine. Following supplementation, standing vertical jump ability was greater, and bench press and squat performance increased by around 11 per cent.

- Bosco (1997) investigated the effect of creatine supplementation on performance of a 45-second continuous jumping protocol and an intensive run to exhaustion. Performance capacity in the jumping test improved by 7 per cent during the first 15 seconds and 12 per cent during the second 15 seconds. Run time to exhaustion improved by 13 per cent.
- Volek (1997) showed an improvement in squat jump performance using 30 per cent of the subjects' 1RM (one-repetition maximum) as a load, and also found an increase in the number of bench-press reps to fatigue.
- Ekblom (1996) found a beneficial effect in high-intensity, intermittent exercise. However, when the subjects ran for 20 minutes the weight gained through supplementation decreased performance.
- Earnest (1995) noted significant increases in absolute bench-press strength, total lifting volume and muscular endurance after supplementation.

The argument against

There has recently been a certain amount of 'bad press' concerning creatine supplementation. Some of the issues that have been raised are as follows.

WEIGHT GAIN

A consistent side-effect in research has been weight gain (typically 0.5–2.0 kg). This is thought to be due primarily to extra water being taken into the muscles; therefore it is particularly important to maintain adequate hydration during supplementation. Water retention is possibly not the only cause of weight gain, though: supplementation may actually stimulate muscle growth, which would increase body weight. The weight gained does not, however, appear to counteract the beneficial effects of creatine supplementation.

SUPPRESSION OF THE BODY'S OWN CREATINE SYNTHESIS

Greater dietary intake of creatine via supplementation causes a suppression of the body's own creatine production. This is because the body's creatine demands are being met solely through the diet. However, this suppression does not seem to extend beyond the supplementation period and once supplementation is ended, normal production is resumed in several weeks (as noted by Walker, 1979).

INCREASED STRESS ON THE LIVER/KIDNEYS

Concern has been raised over the possibility that supplementation may place extra stress on the liver and kidneys. This is because the large quantity of creatine taken when supplementing using a loading and maintenance protocol means that the kidneys have to work harder to clear any unabsorbed creatine from the bloodstream. However, long-term, high-dose supplementation should have no effect on liver and kidney function in healthy people, although those with liver and kidney conditions should be aware of the risks involved if they are considering taking creatine.

MUSCLE CRAMPING

The cause of muscle cramps is one of the most hotly debated areas in sports medicine and science. They are often associated with periods of high-volume, high-intensity training, and their likelihood may increase when exercising in the heat. Ample fluid intake and a balanced diet rich in electrolytes (salts) and minerals can often reduce the occurrence of muscle cramps, so dehydration and a poor diet may increase the risk.

There have been reports of increased muscle cramping associated with creatine supplementation. One possible explanation for this is based around the fact that during the early phases of creatine supplementation extra water is taken up into the muscle cells. If hydration status is not maintained this could, potentially, increase the likelihood of cramps. However, as the exact cause of muscle cramps is unknown it is difficult to attribute it to any one factor, let alone creatine. Also, there appear to be no scientific reports that relate creatine to cramping.

MUSCLE STRAINS/PULLS

Reports from athletes and coaches have suggested an increased incidence and severity of muscle strains/pulls following creatine supplementation – these have not been supported by research. Unrealistic training expectations, such as massive increases in training volume and/or intensity following supplementation, may be a likely cause of injury rather than any underlying physiological factor relating to creatine.

LONG-TERM SIDE-EFFECTS

Creatine is still a relatively new supplement, even though it is one of the most popular and most celebrated. Therefore, even though investigations are being carried out into the effects of long-term, high-dosage use, it has not been around long enough for scientists/doctors to say that it is safe to use for long periods of time. Unfortunately, there is no knowing whether taking large doses of creatine for long periods will cause any unwanted side-effects in the future.

However, based on current data, and the informed decisions of doctors and sports scientists, creatine appears to be a safe and effective performance enhancer, as long as it is taken in the way recommended. Any risks associated with the long-term usage of creatine are linked to the ingestion of large volumes of creatine for sustained periods.

LEGALITY

As creatine is found in meat eaters' diets, it would be difficult to determine where excess amounts were being ingested from. Therefore, it is not currently in violation of any sports governing body's rules. Additionally, the IOC, as mentioned above, does not include creatine on its list of banned substances.

Protein supplements

For many years experts, coaches and competitors have debated the question of whether or not athletes – particularly those trying to gain muscle mass – should consume extraordinary amounts of protein in their diets. There are literally hundreds of protein supplements on the market and they consistently hold their place among the top sellers. But are the millions of pounds handed over for these products being spent wisely or just 'peed down the pan'?

What are they?

Protein is essential for all life. It comprises about 15 per cent of the body weight of a human and is found primarily in muscle. Although there are many different proteins, they are all made up of amino acids. Our bodies can make proteins from amino acids, but they can only produce some of the necessary amino acids. Those that cannot be made in the body must be obtained from the diet.

What do they do?

Protein is essential for growth and is used within the body to build new tissue and replace old, worn-out tissue such as muscles. Although protein can be used as an energy source, the actual contribution to overall energy production is normally very small. During short-duration exercise (sprinting, weightlifting) the contribution from protein is negligible, regardless of the intensity of the exercise. Longer-duration exercise (distance running, cycling) may be partially fuelled by protein, but the contribution is still small at approximately 2–5 per cent. However, there are situations when the energy contribution may be higher; these include times when carbohydrate stores are low. Even in such cases, however, the contribution of protein is probably 10 per cent at most.

The argument for

Regular exercise and training may increase protein needs, the extent to which this occurs being dependent on the type and duration of the exercise undertaken. Protein supplements are generally marketed at the athlete who is trying to increase muscle mass and therefore undertaking a certain amount of resistance training. When attempts are made to increase muscle mass, additional protein may be required to provide sufficient amino acids to maximise protein synthesis. Several scientific studies (Chelsey *et al.*, 1992; Marable *et al.*, 1979; Yarasheki *et al.*, 1993) have concluded that resistance exercise does, indeed, increase protein synthesis, suggesting a need for extra protein in the diet.

Other studies have tried to quantify the actual amount of protein that would be required by strength training athletes in order to optimise muscle growth. Fern *et al.* (1991) reported that when 2 g/kg of protein was consumed each day for four weeks, whole-body protein synthesis increased and significantly more lean mass was achieved than in subjects who consumed their normal diet. So, this evidence seems to point towards strength trained athletes needing more protein in their diets.

The argument against

However, the study by Fern *et al.* (1991) also found an increase in amino acid oxidation, which suggests that the protein intake of 2 g/kg per day actually exceeded the amount that was needed for muscle growth. Tarnopolsky *et al.* (1992) supported this by reporting that a protein intake of 2.4 g/kg per day did not increase protein synthesis more than an intake of 1.4 g/kg per day, but the larger intake did increase amino acid oxidation. Therefore, the extra intake was not being used for increasing muscle mass.

The recommendations for protein intake by athletes is generally between 1.2 and 1.8 g/kg per day. However, a beginner may need slightly more in the first couple of weeks (Lemon, 1992). The only athletes who realistically need more than this are children and adolescents, who need extra protein to allow for growth and may need up to 2 g/kg per day. Most athletes will meet their protein needs through their diets, although people following energy-restriction diets or strict vegetarian diets may need to address their protein intake. One recommendation for athletes who believe they are not consuming adequate protein is dry milk powder (casein), which will provide all the necessary amino acids at a fraction of the cost of protein supplements. There is simply no scientific evidence to suggest that the protein in supplements is more effective for athletes than the protein in ordinary foods.

Where do they occur naturally?

Protein is found in many foods such as dairy products, fish, meat, poultry, soya products, meat substitutes (such as Quorn), beans, nuts, bread and cereals. However, a lot of these foods tend to be high in fat or cooked in ways that increase fat content, so be careful if you are watching your weight!

Thermogenic aids/fat burners

What are they?

Supplements that will apparently help you to lose body weight effortlessly. The word 'thermogenic' literally means 'to produce heat', and something that causes you to burn more calories is said to have a thermogenic effect. These supplements often contain stimulants such as caffeine, ephedrine or guarana. Other supplements touted as 'fat burners' contain substances like carnitine, chromium and pyruvate.

What do they do?

These substances claim to metabolise fat and use it as a fuel source, therefore draining your fat stores and making you leaner! Some of these supplements may be helpful in suppressing appetite and controlling food cravings. Stimulant-type supplements are responsible for decreasing your appetite and increasing your calorie utilisation over a short period of time. However, they do nothing to affect your basal metabolic rate (BMR), which is the amount of calories you use at rest.

The argument for

Although a combination of sensible dieting and exercise is known to be the most effective way to reduce body fat, the thought that 'popping a few pills' may help you do it faster can be very alluring. None of these supplements, however, is able to simply melt away your fat deposits.

Stimulant substances function to slightly increase energy expenditure and suppress appetite, and have been shown to reduce weight in obese subjects. Examples of substances tested include caffeine, guarana and ephedra. Guarana is found in many weight loss products, while ephedra is present in almost all 'fat-burning' products; both of these are naturally occurring, herbal equivalents of caffeine and therefore act on the central nervous system to elicit the effects described above. However, both have also been linked with the side-effects detailed below.

Chromium is one of the most popular supplements used for weight loss. It plays a vital role in carbohydrate metabolism and may help control blood sugar levels, so helping to reduce cravings. Pyruvate is another supplement commonly associated with weight loss as it may enhance the amount of fat lost while following a calorie-controlled diet. This seems to be due to its ability to slightly increase the metabolic rate and, hence, the number of calories used per day while consuming it.

Carnitine is a supplement that does have some scientific backing to its claims. Human muscles contain a large amount of carnitine and its primary function is to transport fat to the sites in the muscles where it can be used for energy. So, the theory is that if you increase the amount of carnitine in the muscle, you will increase the amount of fat being used and so start to drain your fat stores.

The argument against

In reality, there is no magic pill or powder that will accelerate body fat loss. Few nutritional supplements that are advertised as able to 'burn fat' have ever been proven to do so. In fact, the only true thermogenic aids are water, oxygen, exercise and proper nutrition.

Only two – chromium and pyruvate – have undergone rigorous scientific scrutiny, and this was in obese subjects not athletes. Other studies show that carnitine has no effect on body fat, fat metabolism or performance; there are also those that show positive effects. In fact, studies have shown that the carnitine molecules ingested as supplements are too large to be able to enter the muscle cell anyway, so they are completely ineffective!

Ephedrine is a banned substance and a drug rather than a nutritional supplement. However, it occurs naturally in many herbal products such as ephedra (e.g. Ma Huang and Chinese Ephedra), mentioned above. Ephedrine has a structure similar to that of amphetamines and there is no data on its ability to reduce weight in healthy, non-obese individuals. It can cause side-effects such as tremors and nervousness, and can also increase heart rate and blood pressure. Even more serious side-effects that have been reported include myocardial infarctions, strokes, seizures, psychosis and death. Combining ephedrine with other stimulants, such as caffeine, increases the potency of the stimulant and the chances of adverse events. Long-term stimulant use can also depress your BMR, meaning that you are more likely to end up gaining weight rather than losing it, due to the following factors.

- **Dehydration** – stimulants have a diuretic effect, which increases the risk of dehydration and inhibits fat metabolism.
- **Muscle breakdown** – restricting calories and using stimulants increases the production of stress hormones, which convert muscle tissue into glucose to raise blood sugar levels. Reducing muscle mass effectively lowers the BMR and increases the risk of fatigue, injury and illness.
- **Poor performance** – elevated stress levels and broken-down muscle tissue result in poor performance and a reduced ability to exercise, which will result in a further drop in the BMR.

Recipe and snack ideas

Moving away from all the talk of supplements, let's get back to more 'natural' dietary concerns. Here are some ideas for quick, easy and nutritious (and sometimes portable) snacks.

Sandwiches

Sandwiches are a convenient component of packed meals to take to school or college, and indeed to training and competitions. All breads are an excellent source of carbohydrate. When making sandwiches, use a small amount of low-fat spread. Avoid using spread at all with moist sandwich fillings.

Serving suggestions

- Tri-wedges – include a third slice of bread in the centre of the sandwich
- Toast wedges – toast the bread to make a hot snack or use a sandwich maker
- Pocket wedges – filled pitta breads
- Roll wedges – place fillings on naan breads and roll up
- Continental wedges – try different breads such as rye, pumpernickel, bagels and bread sticks
- Cut slices of bread thickly

Filling ideas

- Lean roast meat with pickle, mustard and chutney with salad
- Chicken or turkey with reduced-fat mayo or cranberry sauce – add mixed salad and chopped walnuts
- Reduced-fat cheese and lean ham – add celery, lettuce, grated carrot and/or tomato
- Cottage or ricotta cheese with dried fruit, chopped walnuts and mixed salad
- Low-fat houmous with cucumber and grated carrot
- Tuna in brine or salmon with salad, spring onions or cucumber

- Marmite with cottage cheese and salad
- Cottage cheese with fruit
- Ham, cottage or ricotta cheese and pineapple
- Banana and raisin
- Low-fat pâté, salmon or tuna paste
- Low-fat cream cheese and tomato
- Grilled bacon, lettuce and tomato
- Chopped chicken and sweetcorn with low-calorie dressing

Toppings for toast, muffins, bagels and crumpets

- Spaghetti, baked beans or tinned ravioli
- Jam, syrup or honey
- Grilled low-fat cheese and pineapple
- Mashed banana and cinnamon
- Low-fat cheese and lean ham
- Scrambled egg and tomato sauce
- Low-fat cream cheese and banana
- Chopped egg mixed with plain yoghurt
- Sardines/mackerel in tomato sauce

Desserts

- Fresh or tinned fruits
- Low-fat yoghurt or fromage frais
- Low-fat tinned or home-made rice pudding or custard
- Low-fat mousse
- Low-fat ice cream
- Sorbet
- Jelly

Baked potato fillings

- Mexican tuna – tinned tomatoes, red pepper, onion and tuna
- Cheesy bean potatoes – baked beans, low-fat grated cheese and pepper
- Mushroom toppers – onion, mushroom, tomato, basil and black pepper
- Mushroom and beans – sliced mushrooms, onions and baked beans
- Chicken and sweetcorn – chicken, sweetcorn, fromage frais, mustard, pepper and parsley
- Fishy potato – tinned fish in tomato sauce, chopped pepper and tomato
- Bacon delight – lean grilled bacon, grilled mushrooms and tomatoes

More potato ideas

- New potato salad – new potatoes in natural yoghurt with spring onions and sweetcorn
- Minted potato salad – new potatoes in low-fat yoghurt, garlic, cucumber and mint
- Hot potato salad – boiled new potatoes in low-fat yoghurt, garlic, onion, wholegrain mustard, curry paste; sprinkle with a little low-fat grated cheese and bake until hot throughout

The Concept

Lilleshall Sports Injury and Human Performance Centre has been providing advice and giving practical support to elite rugby players for many years. This continues today but now this specialised programme is available to anyone who is serious about achieving peak performance.

How it Works

Pro-Fit clients stay at the Lilleshall National Sports Centre for five days. They undergo an initial fitness and health assessment. They then follow an individually tailored programme under the close supervision of their personal trainer and alongside the elite professional sports people at Lilleshall.

Pro-Fit packages include full board and accommodation in modern, well-appointed rooms at Lilleshall.

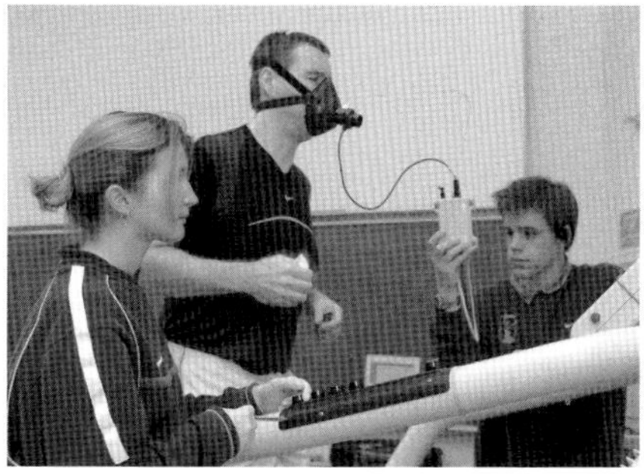

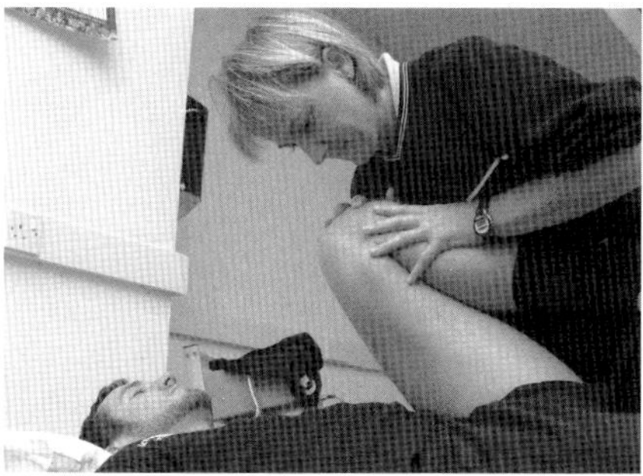

The Programme

Fitness programmes include work to improve endurance, strength and flexibility. Training schedules include circuit training in our fully equipped gym, swimming sessions and mountain biking in and around the idyllic rural setting of Lilleshall. Expert advice on diet and nutrition complement the programme and a certificate of attendance is presented along with a comprehensive information pack on completion.

How to Book

Simply call +44(0)1952 605 828 or e-mail info@lilleshall.com and request a Pro-Fit application form. This form includes a brief questionnaire, which ascertains your current level of fitness and helps us to work out the ideal Pro-Fit package for your specific needs. We will then contact you for your stay at Lilleshall.

AFTERWORD

We hope that the information in this book makes sense to you and will help you to realise whatever goals you set yourself. If we were to summarise the key elements that make up the core of your programme they would be as follows.

Plan ...

... carefully and set realistic objectives for yourself.

Review ...

... constantly by maintaining your progress chart. If you have reached a plateau then it is time to change your routine.

Observe ...

... others at work and yourself to ensure that proper form is maintained.

Communicate

Tell someone close to you what you are up to and involve him or her in the project to help you in the low times that are sure to come.

Enjoy

It is OK to enjoy yourself. Be proud of what you achieve and take it on to the field with you so that you can get the most out of your rugby.

APPENDIX: FOOD AND DRINK DATA

TABLE A.1 The calorific content of alcoholic drinks

Drink	Quantity	Calories
BEERS/LAGERS		
Amstel	1 pint	165
Becks	1 bottle (12oz/340ml)	145
Budweiser	1 bottle (12oz/340ml)	135
Budweiser Light	1 bottle (12oz/340ml)	100
Carling Black Label	1 pint	256
Coors	1 pint	220
Coors Light	1 pint	170
Fosters	1 pint	240
Grolsch	1 bottle (12 oz/340 ml)	150
Guinness	1 pint	245
Harp	1 pint	227
Heineken	1 pint	265
Kronenburg	1 pint	245
Lowenbrau	1 bottle (12 oz/340 ml)	155
Miller	1 bottle (12 oz/340 ml)	140
Miller Lite	1 bottle (12 oz/340 ml)	105
Pilsner	1 bottle (12 oz/340 ml)	155
Red Stripe	1 pint	245
Rolling Rock Premium	1 bottle (12 oz/340 ml)	120
WINES		
Champagne	1 glass (4 oz/110 ml)	85
Dry white	1 glass (4 oz/110 ml)	75
Sweet white	1 glass (4 oz/110 ml)	105
Red	1 glass (4 oz/110 ml)	80
SPIRITS/LIQUEURS		
Baileys	1 measure (37.5 ml)	115
Brandy	1 shot (1 oz/30 ml)	65
Cointreau	1 shot (1.5 oz/45 ml)	190
Drambuie	1 shot (1.5 oz/45 ml)	190
Gin	1 shot (1 oz/30 ml)	65
Rum	1 shot (1 oz/30 ml)	65
Tequila	1 shot (1 oz/30 ml)	65
Vodka	1 shot (1 oz/30 ml)	65
Whisky	1 shot (1 oz/30 ml)	65

TABLE A.2 What 50 g of carbohydrate looks like*

Food	50 g serving	Food	50 g serving
Fruit juice	1 pint	Pitta bread	2
Full sugar fruit squash	3 glasses	Ryvita	9
Milk	2 pints	Crispbreads	15 small/6 large
Flavoured milk	1 pint	Rice cakes	6 thick/10 thin
Soft drinks	1 pint	Cereal bars	3
3% carbohydrate drink	1670 ml	Muesli bars	2.5
6% carbohydrate drink	833 ml	Malt loaf	3 slices
7.5% carbohydrate drink	666 ml	Sweetcorn	10 tbsps/2 cobs
Fruit in heavy syrup	1 small tin	Baked potatoes	1 large
Fruit in juice	1 large tin	Ravioli	8 tbsps
Apples	4	Rice (boiled)	4 tbsps
Oranges	4	Pasta	8 tbsps
Bananas	2	Noodles	8 tbsps
Pears	3	Tinned spaghetti in tomato sauce	8 tbsps/1 large can
Dried apricots	20	Baked beans	7 tbsps/1 large can
Raisins	4 tbsps	Rice (fried)	6 tbsps
Bran flakes	1 large bowl	Pizza	0.25 deep pan
Weetabix	5 biscuits	Fromage frais	2 tubs
Cornflakes	1 large bowl	Low-fat fruit yoghurt	2 pots
Muesli	1 medium bowl	Plain sweet biscuits	9
Bagels	1	Jaffa cakes	6
Bread	4 slices	Jam/marmalade	9 tsps
Crumpets	3	Honey/syrup	9 tsps
English muffins	2	Fruit pastilles	2 tubes
Croissants	2	Jelly babies	1 medium packet (60 g)
Bread rolls	2	Iced fruit bun	1.5

* Table of foods and the portion sizes needed to provide 50 g of carbohydrate

TABLE A.3 What 10 g of protein looks like*

Food	10 g serving	Food	10 g serving
Fruit juice	1 pint	Pitta bread	2
Grilled fish	50 g (cooked weight)	Cottage cheese	70 g
Tuna/salmon	50 g	Semi-skimmed milk	300 ml
Lean beef/lamb	35 g (cooked weight)	Muesli	1 cup (100 g)
Veal	35 g (cooked weight)	Wholemeal bread	4 slices (120 g)
Turkey/chicken	40 g (cooked weight)	Cooked brown rice	3 cups (400 g)
Eggs	2 small	Cooked lentils	0.75 cup (150 g)
Low-fat fromage frais	150 g	Cooked kidney beans	0.75 cup (150 g)
Reduced-fat cheese	30 g	Baked beans	1 small can (200 g)
Low-fat yoghurt	200 g	Tofu	120 g
Seeds (i.e. sesame)	60 g	Nuts	60 g
Wheat bran flake cereal	3 cups (90 g)	Cooked pasta/noodles	2 cups (300 g)

* Table of foods and the portion sizes needed to provide 10 g of protein

Fast-food hell?

It is one of God's little jests that lots of the stuff that tastes great is not much benefit to us. Check out the following stats on fast-food values.

TABLE A.4 Fast-food hell?

Product	Calories	Fat (g)	Carbs (g)	Protein (g)
McDONALDS				
Hamburger	260	9	34	13
Cheeseburger	320	13	35	15
Quarter Pounder	420	21	37	23
Quarter Pounder w/Cheese	530	30	38	28
Big Mac	560	31	45	26
Crispy Chicken Deluxe	500	25	43	26
Fish Fillet Deluxe	560	28	54	23
Grilled Chicken Deluxe	440	20	38	27
Small Fries	210	10	26	3

TABLE A.4 Fast-Food – continued

Product	Calories	Fat (g)	Carbs (g)	Protein (g)
Large Fries	450	22	57	6
Super Fries	540	26	68	8
Chicken McNuggets (4)	190	11	10	12
Chicken McNuggets (6)	290	17	15	18
Chicken McNuggets (9)	430	26	23	27
Hot Mustard	60	3.5	7	1
Honey Mustard	50	4.5	3	0
Light Mayonnaise	40	4	0	0
Garden Salad	35	0	7	2
Grilled Chicken Salad Deluxe	120	1.5	7	21
Croutons	50	1.5	7	2
Caesar Salad	160	14	7	2
Ranch Dressing	230	21	10	1
Egg McMuffin	290	12	27	17
Sausage McMuffin	360	23	26	13
Sausage & Egg McMuffin	440	28	27	19
English Muffin	140	2	25	4
Sausage	170	16	0	6
Scrambled Eggs (2)	160	11	1	13
Hash Browns	130	8	14	1
Pancakes Plain	310	7	53	9
Pancakes w/Margarine and Syrup	580	16	100	9
Apple Danish	360	16	51	5
Cinnamon Roll	400	20	47	7
Strawberry Sundae	290	7	50	7
Hot Caramel Sundae	360	10	61	7
Baked Apple Pie	260	13	34	3
Chocolate Chip Cookie	170	10	22	2
McDonald's Cookies	180	5	32	3
Vanilla Shake (small)	360	9	59	11
Chocolate Shake (small)	360	9	60	11
Strawberry Shake (small)	360	9	60	11
Orange Juice	80	0	20	1
Coca-Cola (small)	150	0	40	0
Coca-Cola (medium)	210	0	58	0
Coca-Cola (large)	310	0	86	0
Diet Coke (any size)	0	0	0	0

TABLE A.4 Fast-Food – continued

Product	Calories	Fat (g)	Carbs (g)	Protein (g)
Sprite (small)	150	0	39	0
Sprite (medium)	210	0	56	0
Sprite (large)	310	0	83	0
BURGER KING				
Whopper Sandwich	640	39	45	27
Whopper Sandwich with Cheese	730	46	46	33
Double Whopper	870	56	45	46
Double Whopper with Cheese	960	63	46	52
Whopper Jr	420	24	29	21
Whopper Jr with Cheese	460	28	29	23
Hamburger	330	15	28	20
Cheeseburger	380	19	28	23
Double Cheeseburger	600	36	28	41
Double Cheeseburger + Bacon	640	39	28	44
BK Big Fish	700	41	56	26
BK Broiler	550	29	41	30
Chicken Sandwich	710	43	54	26
Chicken Tenders (8 pieces)	310	17	19	21
Broiled Chicken Salad	200	10	7	21
Garden Salad no dressing	100	5	7	6
Side Salad no dressing	60	3	4	3
French Fries (medium/salted)	370	20	43	5
Coated French Fries	340	17	43	0
Onion Rings	310	14	41	4
Dutch Apple Pie	300	15	39	3
Vanilla Shake (medium)	300	6	53	9
Chocolate Shake (medium)	320	7	54	9
Coca Cola Classic (medium)	280	0	70	0
Diet Coke (medium)	0	0	0	0
Sprite (medium)	260	0	66	0
Tropicana Orange Juice	140	0	33	2
Coffee	5	0	1	0
Milk (2% low fat)	130	5	12	8
Croissant w/Sausage, Egg, Cheese	600	46	25	22
Hash Browns	220	12	25	2

TABLE A.4 Fast-Food – continued

Product	Calories	Fat (g)	Carbs (g)	Protein (g)
Lettuce	0	0	0	0
Tomato	5	0	1	0
Onion	5	0	1	0
Pickles	0	0	0	0
Ketchup	15	0	4	0
Mustard	0	0	0	0
Mayonnaise	210	23	0	0
Tartar Sauce	180	19	0	0
Bull's Eye BBQ Sauce	20	0	5	0
Bacon Bits	15	1	0	1
Croutons	30	1	4	0
Thousand Island Dressing	140	12	7	0
French Dressing	140	10	11	0
Ranch Dressing	180	19	2	0
Blue Cheese Dressing	160	16	1	2
Honey	90	0	23	0
BBQ Sauce	35	0	9	0
Sweet/Sour Sauce	45	0	11	0
DOMINO'S PIZZA				
Thin Crust Cheese (one-sixth)	255	11	28	11
Deep Dish Cheese (one-sixth)	463	20	55	18
Thin Crust w/peppers, olives, mushrooms (one-sixth)	271	12	29	12
Deep Dish w/peppers, olives, mushrooms (one-sixth)	480	21	56	19
Thin Crust Pepperoni (one-sixth)	354	19	30	16
Deep Dish Pepperoni (one-sixth)	563	28	56	23
Thin Crust Cheese (one-quarter)	273	12	30	12
Deep Dish Cheese (one-quarter)	467	21	52	18
Cheese Pizza (1 pizza)	591	27	65	23
Barbeque Wings (1)	50	2	2	6
Hot Wings (1)	45	2	1	5
Breadsticks (1)	78	3	11	2
Cheesy Bread (1)	103	5	11	3
Small Garden Salad	22	0	4	1
Large Garden Salad	39	0	8	2

TABLE A.4 Fast-Food – continued

Product	Calories	Fat (g)	Carbs (g)	Protein (g)
KFC				
Wing with skin	121	8	1	12
Breast with skin	251	11	1	37
Breast without skin	169	4	1	31
Thigh with skin	207	12	2	18
Thigh without skin	106	6	1	13
Drumstick with skin	97	4	1	15
Drumstick without skin	67	2	1	11
Whole wing	140	10	5	9
Crispy Strips (3)	261	16	10	20
Chunky Chicken Pot Pie	770	42	69	29
Hot Wings Pieces (6)	471	33	18	27
Original Recipe Chicken Sandwich	497	22	46	29
Value BBQ Chicken Sandwich	256	8	28	17
Kentucky Nuggets (6)	284	18	15	16
Corn on the Cob	190	3	34	5
Green Beans	45	2	7	1
BBQ Baked Beans	190	3	33	6
PIZZA HUT				
Thin 'n' Crispy (1 slice)	210	9	21	12
Pan (1 slice)	300	14	30	15
Stuffed Crust (1 slice)	380	11	49	21
Buffalo Wings mild (5)	200	12	0	23
Buffalo Wings hot (4)	210	12	4	22
Garlic Bread (1 slice)	150	8	16	3
Bread Stick (1 slice)	130	4	20	3
Bread Stick Dip Sauce	30	0.5	5	0
Spaghetti w/Marinara	490	6	91	18
Spaghetti w/Meat Sauce	600	13	98	23
Spaghetti w/Meatballs	850	24	120	37
Cavatini Pasta	480	14	66	21
Cavatini Supreme Pasta	560	19	73	24
Ham and Cheese Sandwich	550	21	57	33
Supreme Sandwich	640	28	62	34
Apple Dessert Pizza (1 slice)	250	4.5	48	3
Cherry Dessert Pizza (1 slice)	250	4.5	47	3

FURTHER READING

Further reading

Arnold's Bodybuilding For Men

Authors: Arnold Schwarzenegger and Bill Dobbins
Published by: Fireside (reprint edition, 12 October 1984)
ISBN: 0671531638
Summary: Ah, now you may be surprised to see this find its way into this book's selection of recommended reading. Surely Arnie is a musclebound poser? Think again – this book is packed full of good basic information. Surprisingly, protein shakes, supplements of dubious value, and exotic weight training routines are notable by their absence. Great book for dipping in to.

Circuit Training

Authors: Morgan and Adamson
Published by: Bell
ISBN: 0713507659
Summary: The first and still the best – from the *originators* of circuit training. Vital if you want all-over fitness. This book is now out of print and therefore difficult to track down. However, if you can get hold of a copy, it will be a fantastic source of information.

The Complete Guide to Strength Training

Author: Anita Bean
Published by: A & C Black
ISBN: 0713660406
Summary: A great book if you have a little more time on your hands or just want some more variety. Be aware, though, that it has its basis in the bodybuilding and 'reshaping' world, whose objectives differ from those of this book.

Essentials of Strength Training and Conditioning

Authors: Baechle and Earle
Published by: Human Kinetics
ISBN: 0736000895
Summary: The most comprehensive work ever written on this subject.

Food for Fitness

Author: Anita Bean
Published by: A & C Black
ISBN: 0713663863
Summary: A good, practical guide. Covers topics such as eating on the run, boosting your energy, healthy snacks, healthy weight loss, and recipes such as snack bars and pasta.

Know the Game: Weightlifting, Powerlifting, Weight Training (three separate booklets)

Authors: Various
Published by: A & C Black
ISBN: Various
Summary: Backed by the British Weight Lifting Association. Ideal for the beginner. Three simple, clear introductions.

SAQ Rugby
Author: Alan Pearson
Published by: A & C Black
ISBN: 0713659491
Summary: Recommended by the RFU Fitness Adviser.

Sports Training Principles
Author: Frank W. Dick
Published by: A & C Black
ISBN: 0713658657
Summary: Possibly the best book ever written on the subject – quite superb. An advanced version of the same author's *Training Theory* (see below).

Strength Training
Author: Max Jones
Published by: British Athletic Federation
ISBN: 0851340970
Summary: Clear explanations and illustrations. A superb introduction – especially if you train alone.

Strength Training Anatomy
Author: Frederic Delavier
Published by: Human Kinetics
ISBN: 0736041850
Summary: Full-colour illustrations of the muscles used during the exercises. Brilliant illustrations – the only drawback is that it is aimed at bodybuilders rather than athletes. Well worth a glance though and a very nice coffee table book.

Training Theory

Author: Frank W. Dick

Published by: British Athletic Federation

ISBN: 0851341055

Summary: An excellent introduction to the ideas that govern training for fitness. If you want to understand what you are doing, this is for you.

The Weightlifting Encyclopedia: A Guide to World-Class Performance

Author: Arthur Drechsler

Published by: A is A Communications

ISBN: 0965917924

Summary: This covers absolutely everything you could ever want to know about Olympic lifting. If you are going to use O-lifts as a core part of your training, then this is fabulous reading.

Weight Training and Lifting

Author: John Lear

Published by: A & C Black

ISBN: 0713656743

Summary: The official British Weight Lifting Association textbook. Excellent

USEFUL CONTACTS

Conrad Phillips runs individually tailored courses for clubs and individuals, and can be contacted via *email: conrad.phillips@btinternet.com*

Lilleshall Human Performance Centre has been providing applied sports science and sports injury rehabilitation services for the past 16 years. We are home to the UK's only residential sports injury rehabilitation centre:
tel: 01952 605828
email: info@lilleshall.com

For coaches who can provide more guidance on speed development you can contact the sprint coach at your local athletics club, or try the following organisations:

Amateur athletic association
Under 'development' on their website they have details of regional development co-ordinators and clubs.
tel: 0121 452 1500
website: www.englandathletics.org.uk
Regional contacts:

Northern Ireland Athletic Federation	tel: 028 906 02707
Scottish Athletics Federation	tel: 0131 317 7320
Athletic Association of Wales	tel: 01633 416 633
North of England Athletics Association	tel: 0113 246 1835
Midland Counties Athletics Association	tel: 0121 456 1896
South of England Athletics Association	tel: 0208 664 7244

UK Athletics
Under 'clubs' you will find a great network of athletics clubs close to you
website: *www.ukathletics.net*

For coaches who can provide more guidance on weight training and weight lifting contact:

The British Weight Lifting Association
Lilleshall National Sports Centre
Newport
Shropshire
TF10 9AT
tel: 01952 604201

National Strength and Conditioning Association (NSCA)
An American website packed full of great information
website: www.nsca-lift.org

For advice on finding a physiotherapist specialising in sports medicine:

The Association Of Chartered Physiotherapists in Sports Medicine (ACPSM)
The ACPSM is the clinical interest group recognised by the Chartered Society of Physiotherapy, representing physiotherapists who have an interest and involvement in Sports Physiotherapy. On their website under 'regional reps' you will find contact details of someone near you throughout the UK.
website: www.acpsm.org

INDEX